Dust and Destiny

FIFTEEN SERMONS

By
M. S. RICE

"He knoweth our frame; he remembereth
that we are dust."
"But the mercy of the Lord is from everlasting
to everlasting upon them that fear him."

THE METHODIST BOOK CONCERN
NEW YORK   CINCINNATI   CHICAGO

Printed in the United States of America

First Edition Printed April, 1921
Second Printing, October, 1921
Third Printing, July, 1922
Fourth Printing, January, 1926
Fifth Printing, June, 1929

TO
MY FATHER
CYRUS ROBERT RICE
WHO TAUGHT ME
THE ALPHABET
FROM THE BIBLE
AND LIVED BEFORE ME
THROUGH A LONG LIFE
THE UNFALTERING EXAMPLE
OF A
MINISTER OF THE WORD

44310

CONTENTS

CONTENTS

THESE sermons have been prepared for print from pulpit notes, and have been intentionally made to retain, as far as possible, the phraseology of the preacher rather than that of the writer. They are nothing other than the regular sermons of an ordinary preacher, and cover a fair range of the ordinary service of the pulpit. They have been arranged for publication by the members of the Young Men's Bible Class of our church, and it is their hope that going to a bit larger field than that originally accorded them, may make them somewhat more ministrant in righteousness.

M. S. R.

North Woodward Tabernacle,
    Detroit, 1921.

DUST AND DESTINY

DUST AND DESTINY

"This mortal must put on immortality."—*1 Cor. 15. 53.*

A STRANGELY contradictory choice of words is
woven together in this passage of Scripture from
which our text is taken. Extremes are welded:
corruption and incorruption; mortality and immortality. We know corruption. We know mortality. We were born and raised among them.
They have greeted us everywhere. We have been
in constant fight against them. We have painted
our decaying houses. We have doctored our
staggering, failing, dying mortality to establish
it in the longest run, and push the grave over
behind the farthest horizon. The reason for all
this being that something within us has forever
cried out against corruption and mortality.
Dominant as those things are here on earth,
mankind has gone ever about his destiny in a
confidence that they were not ultimates. We
have shaken them off. We have built them out.
We have felt the pulse of immortality. One time
when David was wrestling with this same thing
he looked up out of his conscious mortality and
said, "Thou knowest our frame; Thou remembereth that we are dust"; and then, as though he
would not be content with such a description,

11

he said, "But the mercy of the Lord is from ever-lasting to everlasting." Dust and destiny. Sometimes the dust gets the better of our thought, and we choke with mortality. Sometimes the destiny of us shakes off the dust, commands our attention, and out of the crumbling things of mortality there rises the confidence of our faith in immortality.

Dust and destiny, that is man. A bit of the earth, and earthly, a breath of God and heaven-born. Somewhere in, and around, and out of that tangled contrariness arises the human problem. "What is man, that thou art mindful of him?" The psalmist dared hurl that question at God because he had his eye on the dust. "When I consider Thy heavens, the moon and the stars which Thou hast ordained, what is man?" That's it; whenever I set myself to looking at dust, bulk counts, and this little handful called to house me has no chance, for there are worlds and stars of it.

I saw Mrs. Maybrick just after she was set free from the prison wherein she had been con-fined in a stone cell for many years. I asked her if she would tell me in the fewest possible words what was the first thought which came to her when she was set free, and she replied in a flash, "Eight feet." I told her I didn't under-stand what she meant, and she replied: "I have been for many years confined in a solid stone cell, eight feet long. I have tramped the floor of that cell till I wore it down by the tireless determination that some day I would get my freedom. I have walked back and forth on my eight-foot journey for days and months and years, until eight feet seem measured into my very existence. When at last they opened the door and told me I could go, I started, and at the end of the first eight feet I turned around, and started back. I had to turn myself about again, only to repeat the same experience at the next eight feet of my way. Again and again that same awful fact of eight feet that I had year by year trampled into my life, presented itself in my way, and to this moment I have to literally force my way across every eight-foot measure in my path."

I am wondering just how thoroughly this dust of my mortality will get itself ground into my soul by the years of my confinement here, and just how long it will take me after the bars of death have been broken down before me, till I can actually go like an immortal. O, this mortal, how very mortal it is anyhow! If you squeeze the destiny out of this dust of me there is naught but despair. I lift my word as a humble preacher of the faith that has forever kept green above the grave of mortality the eternal hope of immortality. I make no hesitancy to say that scientist or no scientist, I consider the machinations of spiritualistic mediums, so called, with their tilting tables, or rapping noises, or what not, as absolute sacrilege against death. Great majestic death has arisen to shut in silent dignity the doors against clamoring mortality, and does not now propose to be abused by those who would forever link life to some sort of mortal impress. For this mortal must put on immortality. Hush the footsteps and the clattering pavements. The dignity of everlasting life in Jesus Christ is what this troubled world needs. There is that in the Christian faith which stands close beside this mortal life of ours, and plants there the immortal hope which has comforted the noble host of the sorrowing all down the ages, and which has enabled men and women to die in victory, and which just the other day set the note of triumph in the last conscious moments of my beloved father as he waited almost impatiently for death.

I want us now to look at this mortal edition of immortality. I have greatly enjoyed the remark of Victor Hugo to an evolutionist who was showing the great Frenchman how he had come from a most lowly descent. "Well," said Hugo, "if you insist that I am a tadpole, I shall insist that I am at least the tadpole of an archangel." I have always believed the comfort the Frenchman got from such an argument was the archangel end of it, rather than the tadpole end of it. Mortality must put on immortality. If mortality is the end of me, what difference does it make, or what care I when it shall end?   If I am to be tossed up to the blind winds in a few years, mere dust to be blown away and scattered to fertilize some field, that hay may grow heavier there to feed some cattle, I had as well died when I was eighty minutes old as to come struggling on to the well-nigh ninety years of my father.

I had two funerals the same day that brought human life to my appreciation as no other experience in all my ministry. We buried one beautiful morning the body of an old man eighty-four years of age. He had been a rarely beautiful character. His life was a finished work. He had been born in poverty, grew to boyhood in that poverty, was apprenticed to a wheelwright, learned the trade well, and became an industrious wagon-maker. By industry and economy he saved out of a long life of hard work enough money to live on in old age, and came down to his last day greatly beloved by his friends, and a man of honor in his Church. We buried him with a feeling that life had made a complete expression in him, and standing beside his grave sang the hymns he loved, and thanked God for a good man.

I went from that grave to another home of sorrow. I found a woman there who had paid that indescribable price we call motherhood, and brought into the world the tiny fragment of mor-

tality that had breathed but a few hours and
passed away. That babe had never so much as
cast a recognizing glance at its mother, had never
swallowed a mouthful of food, had never even
breathed the air of this strenuous world save
to cry out with the pain in its tender lungs. It
wearied to death of mortality ere three days
had gone. I sat beside the father and tried to
say a few words that might find attention for our
faith, and then he and I took the tiny casket on
our knees and rode out to lay the little form
under the sod. As we were coming back he said
to me in a deeply searching way, "Mr. Rice, what
is the use of having lived at all?" It was a hard
question, for it was run up square against my
experience at the grave of what we had all called
a full-chanced life. That father was a mechanic
and had dealt with mathematics enough to catch
the meaning of a figure which flashed to me as
though by Providence out of the darkness of that
hard question he asked. I said to him, that while
I could not any more remember the process of the
argument I yet held the meaning of one of the
basal formulas of calculus. They have a figure
in calculus which looks like a figure eight lying
sidewise, ∞. It means that any finite quantity
in proportion to infinity gives the same result.
It seems queer at first, but is secure in mathematical reasoning, because the second member of
the equation being absolutely without measure

all proportion of any measure whatever is re-
duced to the same significance. He said he saw
the reason for that. Then I said, "Let us now
make a bit of human calculus, with your babe,
and you, or the old man from whose grave I
have just come, or the oldest man who ever lived,
as the point of reckoning. Grant me the second
member of the human equation to be immortality,
and then whatever you put on this mortal side of
the sum, whether it be the eighty-four years of
the last one I have buried or your own thirty
years, or your babe's two days of life, the result
is exactly the same, for after all, the real greatness of any human life is not how long it shall
live on this earth, but rather that it is an immortal soul."

Let us fix now in our meditation the order of
the saying of our text, for the pessimism which
roots itself in decaying mortality, must be met
by the eternal hope which leaps out in the salvation of God. Mortality needs immortality. It
drives men to desperation to sit amid the fast ash-
ing embers of a mortal world and study the ashes,
as testimony of the end. I need not bring now any
argument for mortality. Blind men see it. Deaf
men hear the requiem. Death is bound to break
in. You can't build it out. There is a mistaken
idea about, that the war brought us an extra
amount of dying. It didn't. Death simply came
sooner to some, was all. It would all have come.

The slower foot of death in peace days than in war days, is no release from the certainty of its arrival. Mortality forever chokes us. But this immortal pilgrim we call a man goes marching on. Convince me of mortality and I am ready to consider immortality.

I received a most impressive invitation from a man some time ago asking me to come back to his town where I once had been pastor and attend his funeral which he was sure would be at a near-coming day. He had been for most of his life careless of the claims of religion. Three months before his death he found to his amazement that the body in which he had lived for years to a prime manhood with a health that had conspired to a confident carelessness, was all undermined with a cancer, and he must soon die. When the expert surgeons told him his case, he wrote me one of the most impressive letters I ever received. He made his peace with God, and wrote me several remarkable letters. His death happened at a time that made my attendance impossible, but I went to his home about a week later and found the town in the grip of the death he had accomplished. As I walked up to the home where he had lived my attention was called to some large limbs that had been cut from two elm trees standing beside the porch. He had done it with his own hands, so the hearse could be brought up to the porch. He had made minute arrangements for the care of every detail. He had walked about the streets, by sheer nerve, till the day before he died. He talked religion to everybody he met. That little town never realized mortality and immortality so intricately tangled together, as when that big, stout man was at the task of folding his tent to leave. But he, good fellow, splendid fellow in many ways, had to have the fact of the mortality of him simply ground into his very heart-blood before he could see the reach of his destiny.

There are to-day some short-ranged religious ideas proposed that would bring attention to the high calling of Buddha. He offered annihilation as the reward for good works. Everlasting death, not life, is the high calling of Buddha. Come, all ye weary, where'er ye languish, come here and you shall die forever. That is mortal philosophy to a conclusion. Dust without destiny. Mortality without immortality. The grave our final goal. Nirvana, the fine dream of Theosophy, our modern edition of Buddhism. How the dust of it all chokes us down. How sadly the fact of mortality is pressed in upon our hearts.

I would stand now close beside the pessimism springing from mortality to declare my Christian faith, that this mortal shall put on immortality. Not death but life is to be the conclusion of the whole matter. I believe through all the years the most eloquent address I ever heard was

delivered by that eccentric but great preacher,
Sam Jones. It was on why he believed in immortality. In the course of the address he turned
most impressively to tell of the day his mother
died. He was but a lad. The loss of a mother to
a boy broke over his soul. He faced suddenly
then as a man, come on forty years past that
parting, the mortal fact in it all, and said something like this, "She has been buried under the
sod of Alabama for forty years. If I were to go
down there to-morrow, and gently lift the earth
off her precious body, and disinter her bones, I
suppose I could gather all there is of her there in
my two hands. And as I would stand there looking at that handful of dirt and mold I would say,
'Great God, is that all that is left of my precious
mother?' And there with such pitiful evidences
of 'dust to dust, ashes to ashes, earth to earth,'
would come resounding this great message of
our faith, 'This corruption shall put on incorruption, and this mortal shall put on immortality.'"
And holding still that handful of clay, he said
he would lift up his eyes on high and say,
"Thanks, thanks be unto God, Who giveth us the
victory through our Lord Jesus Christ." Can
anyone think of a better message than that to give
to as mortal a world as is this?

> "How does the rivulet find its way?
> How does the flower know its day,
> And ope its cup to catch the ray?

"*I see* the germ in the sunlight reach,
And the nestling knows the old bird's speech,
I do not know who is there to teach.

"*I see* the hare through the thicket glide,
And stars through the trackless spaces ride,
I do not see who is there to guide.

"*He is* eyes for all who is eyes for the mole,
See motion goes to its rightful goal,
O God, I can trust far the human soul."

I sat in the Sistine Chapel in Rome one day, where I had been often before just merely looking at the art which was stuck on its well-smoked gloomy walls. This day I sat looking, but seeing nothing, for I was thinking through the wailing sad description I had been reading of the rendition of the Miserere in this famous place of service. They make studied setting for its impressiveness there. The desolation of it all is enforced on the hearers. The plaintive old Psalm is set in ever increasing wail, as at the end of each musical pulse another candle is snuffed out, until at last with every light gone, and darkness thus made doubly-dark they cry out the closing conclusion of it all, "The world and the lust thereof pass away."

I attended the memorial service of one of the lodges. They had a cluster of lights representing those who had died. The hall was radiant in the light of those men alone. The secretary stood solemnly to call the name of each man three times. After waiting vainly for any response the lights went out, one after another, until at last we sat in the enforced darkness of the absent. Impressive as it all was, it is not for such miserere to intone our story. The message of Christianity will not quench a single light that glows upon the human altar. It rather walks boldly into the gloom which death has ever sought to enshroud our race with, and sets there the gleam of a hope that cannot be quenched. The light of destiny is upon our faces. Upon these mundane shores where often the shadows of darkness cling round us, we have a message for mankind. It is no mere spiritualistic seance to tell us a world-flavored sin-covered message from some who strive to say that life there is very much like life here. If such were the case a throng would arise to flee from it for relief. We are looking for a better life, and the word of this great Book of God founds it upon righteousness. "He that doeth the will of God abideth forever." We will find our immortality sweetened forever in the unmixed beauty and purity of Him whom we shall see in His beauty, and we shall be like Him, for we shall see Him as He is. O man, woman, it doth not yet appear what we shall be. This mortality is so mortal. Struck with disease. Staggered with temptation. Choked with suffering. Dying with gloating death. But this mortal shall put on immortality. Dust and destiny.

UNREASONABLE UNBELIEF

UNREASONABLE UNBELIEF

"If thou be the Son of God, come down from the cross."
—*Matt. 27. 40.*

To get the setting of that striking passage of Scripture that lays bare one of the most outstanding blunders ever made by careless unbelief, we need to approach it through the containing passage written here by the author of the first Gospel. "They that passed by reviled Him, wagging their heads, and saying, 'Thou that destroyest the temple and buildest it in three days, save Thyself. If Thou be the Son of God come down from the cross.' Likewise also the chief priests, mocking Him, with the scribes and elders said, 'He saved others, Himself He cannot save. If He be the King of Israel, let Him now come down from the cross and we will believe Him. He trusted in God, let Him deliver Him now if He will have Him, for He said, 'I am the Son of God.' The thieves also, which were crucified with Him, cast the same in His teeth."

To me that is one of the most significant passages of all Scripture. There is a boldness about it which makes me shudder. It is a searching revelation of human nature blundering about amid divine things in brazen ignorance. It is

the record of men whose too-small lives make
tragedy of misunderstanding when they stand in
the way of God's goings. "If Thou be the Son
of God come down from the cross." As to what
it may mean in the eternal councils of human
welfare for you to remain on that cross and die
there we are little concerned as we speak thus,
for we talk as only in the light of what we can
see from where we stand. We are little concerned seeing you dying there other than the fact
that divinity is challenged now, and we are ready
for a demonstration. We hold the right to determine how divinity should act on an occasion
about which we know nothing.

How sadly God has forever been misunderstood by men, and how utterly wrong have been
the ideas multitudes have had as to how God
should act. We have made bold to declare what
was the reasonable thing in divine conduct. We
would not hesitate even to write out a schedule
for heaven. Here come some little unbelieving
men, and wagging their proud heads in the confidence of the qualification of their unbelief, dare
make proposals of change, in the most sacred and
tragic scene that was ever set on this earth. "If
Thou be the Son of God!" Man nowhere else, in
all his oft-blundering story, looks to me so presumptuous, as when he arises here, when all
heaven is bending above the world's supreme
crisis, and when God Himself has come up to the

extreme price that human sin had forced, and raising his hand for attention, dares to suggest a change in the scene. There have always been men who have thought they could arrange some reasonable route for God, with reasonable to be defined in their own terms. As for myself I have always carefully endeavored to bring my faith up to situations like this of our text and say, when "God moves in some mysterious way his wonders to perform," I will not criticize, for really I never did expect God to be confined to the narrow horizoned way that from my low-standing place I was able to declare reasonable. Who ever made my little judgment the clearing-house of God's conduct? I know very little of how to go myself. I constantly am confounded at the difficulties of my own life. I am bothered much when asked for advice in the conduct of situations of human relationships about me. I do not therefore feel qualified to go plunging into divine crises with a point of order against the proceedings. I may be able to draw comparatively safe courses on which to sail my little ships about our little lakes, and across our heaving seas. I may be able to hurl my little trains across plains and through hard-hearted mountains for a short season. I may sink a shaft and bring out sparkling treasures from my vaults of nature. With such things I am wont to plume a proud confidence that tempts me to forget that

I have only a temporary hold on all I prize. Some unexpected day something startles me. I look up to discover as with a new vision what a little world this is where I walk and work and weary and die. The breath of eternity blows into my face. Suns and stars in confounding numbers all spread across spaces I cannot even think across, seem now to lie in the palm of Him we call God, and I am standing here so inexpressibly small as to find easy room on a sand grain called earth. Think you when I am thus standing in my true perspective that I would dare raise my little hand and protest or dictate in any sense as to the ways of God? And if I was such a fool as to even dare suggest my plans, do you think I would likewise be so much more a fool as to believe that my suggestion would draw a crisis of judgment in divine conduct?

I read a poem once that caught my soul in meaning. Who wrote it or where I read it, I cannot say, and I have watched for it for years. It was a description of a great cathedral. The wonderful high-hung dome; the long rows of receding arches; the massive columns that reared themselves like pillars to hold up heaven. All the combined splendors of a perfectly worked-out plan which had been brought to its completion by painstaking laborers for years and years slaving at the task, conspired together to throw a spell of wonder over the observer. He heard a rattling noise, and looking down the great aisle saw coming a little curly-headed boy pulling a little iron horse and wagon. So fascinated was he that he was backing his way along, gazing in concentrated interest on his toy, and the little iron-horse rattled across the marble pavement, his complete delight. What avail the greatest dome ever hung mid-sky by an architect, he never even looked into it. What avail the finest arch any mason ever laid up, he never knew it was there. What avail the greatest pillar that ever struck its granite shoulder under a load, he never cared how high it stood. What a picture all that of the larger fact when the cathedral has become a universe and the boy has become a man. There he goes pulling the tiny things of his own making, utterly unconscious that above him and about him is the cathedral of God's plan. Look up, man! Look up, woman! You are lost on your avenues. You are thinking in terms of your factory. You are measuring life at your forge. You are counting value in gold and bonds. You cannot spell God out that way.

That is the setting of our text with infinite tragedy added. Unbelief has made bold to wade through the sorrows of God's suffering, and flinging itself into the most sacred moment that has ever dawned on the world, has lifted up its voice to suggest a new course even for God. And when you actually listen to what it suggests how

foolish the suggestion is. If there had been any
other way, it would not have been for some little
man to have thought out the method to prevent
the death of the Son of God on Calvary. You
may be sure Heaven's Court had thought that
matter all through. Had there been any other
possible way, Jesus Christ not only would have
come down from that Cross, but a thousand
cohorts of angels had rather hung there. God
was not needlessly allowing His only Son to be
nailed to a cross outside Jerusalem. O sinful
suffering men! blind men before your own interests; you may not understand the "Cross on
which the Prince of Glory died," but you do not
need to understand it, and its efficacy does not
hang upon your logic anyhow. "If Thou be the
Son of God, come down from the cross!" Hush
such words, man, for you have mixed your meaning. You have stated the very case from which
there can be no appeal. If He was the Son of
God He could not come down from the cross.
He was on that cross only because He was the
Son of God. Any less sacrifice would not do
there. Because He was the Son of God, He must
stay on that cross and die. Because He was
the Son of God, He not only could not be His
own rescuer, but He could not even be rescued
alive from that place, and His own cry, "My God!
My God! Why hast Thou forsaken Me!" the most
searching, and heart-breaking, and heaven-pierc-

ing cry that ever went up from this earth's suffering, must simply die away in the silence of its
own echoes. Because He was the Son of God,
that one particular cross has come to be the symbol out of a thousand crosses where men had been
put to death, and the Church with quenchless
hope frames its hymns here, and sets a whole
world singing out of its troubles and sorrows:

"In the Cross of Christ I glory,
   Towering o'er the wrecks of time;
All the light of sacred story
   Gathers round its head sublime."

We contemplate this hour from this somewhat
strange approach, the Cross of Christ, emphasiz-
ing two significant facts which I wish to get your
appreciation of. I would note first, that Jesus
could not come down from the cross for the very
conclusive reason these unbelievers stated as
their reason for Him to come down. If He was
the Son of God, He could not in this eternal crisis
come down. This was no time for mere miracle
working. O the tender mysterious power of this
scene of my dying Saviour! I draw back instinc-
tively from any effort to merely contemplate it.
I have heard of a physiologist so enamored of
his studies that he could dissect the heart of his
mother. I draw back from the wonders and
expressions of God as laid bare on Calvary, and
instead of feeling about there for reasons, I stand
enthralled at the love that is "so amazing, so

divine," I have nothing to measure the meaning
with. There is mystery unsolvable which shrouds
that cross from our mortal minds. But still it
"towers above the wrecks of time," and still it
grows in influence and mighty power in a sinful
world needing salvation. That cross marches
right on in its meaning. It wades triumphantly
through an awful sea of discouraging sin. It
beats down the barriers of doubt and disbelief.
Though there still is "offense in the cross," as the
heritage of many in its mystery, still, thank God,
upon its beams are the assurances of God's love
and mercy, and upon it this minute hang not only
the hopes of millions in the faith, but likewise
the offered pardon to every man, woman, and
child who will turn eyes of faith out of the sins
they suffer.

How unapproachable our Lord is there. There
He gives us no example. In many of the things
our Saviour did He merely took His place superior, but in kindred mission to those whom we
call great and good in service. He dared not to
leap suddenly mid-sky at a single bound to take
His place on a whole world's altar. Men would
not have been able to even turn their hearts there.
He would have been left to die there hung round
with shrouds of fanaticism. Christ must not
rush from His baptism straight to His death. He
had a company of apostles to inspire. They were
slow of heart. They must be taught something

of the boundless love and tender divinity of His character, before He could accomplish His death. Three years of Jesus' ministry were drawn out only for our sakes. It was not necessary for Him. His death had been sacrificially as effectual had it been accomplished in the wilderness with John Baptist. But His timid, wondering, dull, human disciples must be slowly led along. He must lay well and deep into their consciences and characters the great measures of His ministry. He patiently therefore showed them life just as divine as humanity could carry. But on Calvary Jesus is alone. I know thieves died there the same day, and many another man found death nailed to a cross. But the significance of Calvary is not in the manner of the death there, but in the meaning of the death. "If Thou be the Son of God, come down from the cross!" Be still, poor blind unbelief! Hold! thou blundering presumptive. You have by such shallow words struck foolishly into the very distinction of the hour. This is the one pedestal on which God's Son hangs absolutely alone. If Christ comes down from that cross, He comes down where men in ordinary experience can crowd around Him, He comes back to the conditions where men can follow Him in type of service. He comes giving cups of cold water, I can do that too. He comes clothing the naked, I can do that too. He comes feeding the hungry, I can do that too. He comes

back being a man. On that cross He is wholly
divine, I am therefore not surprised that His
ear was deaf to their challenge. Men don't seem
even yet to grasp the fact that the cross was the
one objective of Christ's coming. He was aimed
straight at that when He left the Throne. He
did not come to earth to get down from the
cross, He came to earth to be nailed to the cross.
The shadow of that cross had fallen as a symbol
of hope across humanity's eastern sky ever since
sin struck its poison into the veins of our race.
The path of Jesus lay out from Bethlehem with
singing angels and wondering shepherds and
worshiping Wise Men, to Calvary with weeping
friends and hooting mobs and darkening skies.
There was no path by which He could turn aside.
Calvary was no calamity, a mere result of God's
oversight. It was not some mistake of Heaven's
Court that could be corrected by human suggestion. The cross was not a blunder, but was the
most sublime event this sin-troubled world has
ever known; and the most presumptuous thing
man ever did, was when those head-wagging unbelievers came heartlessly there, watching Him
die, and said in their mocking way which pre-
faced their claim with a doubt, "If Thou be the
Son of God! If Thou be! If Thou be the Son of
God come down from the cross."

I ask you to observe for our second consideration now that Jesus Christ did not come to save

Himself. I know of nothing that touches my soul to thanks, as does the fact that Jesus came to save mankind from sin. He did not need to come to save Himself. He was safe, and in voluntary mission He said, "I will lay aside my security here and go there and die to rescue those sinners lost to God!" Those stupid unbelievers who stood to see Him die, said, "He saved others, Himself He cannot save. Come from the cross. Come down from the cross." Did you ever know of a saviour of men who made it the primary business first to look to his own salvation? Who ever made that a qualification for saving life? I heard the brother of a man who wrote his name high on the scroll of human heroism, tell how that dauntless swimmer went back again and again and again, each time against the protest of all his friends, to fight his way out to a wreck and bring ashore those imperiled ones. Seventeen times he made the dangerous trip, and when they supplemented his failing strength by pulling on the rope which was bound about his waist, and helped him get through the mad waves with the last survivor, he fell into unconsciousness from which many hours afterward he awakened just enough to ask as the only concern that could find words at his whitened lips, "Did I do my best? Did I do my best?" Never again was that great strong frame of Spencer able to meet the crisis of life. He couldn't save himself when he

was devoted to saving others. There were
plenty of others there that day who saved themselves. Spencer was saving others. That's the
heart of the fact made infinite in Jesus. The
self-forgetfulness of saviour stands out first.
It was consummate in Christ.

> "We may not know, we cannot tell,
>   What pains He had to bear;
> But we believe it was for us
>   He hung and suffered there.
>
> "*He* died that we might be forgiven,
>   He died to make us good,
> That we might go at last to heaven,
>   Saved by His precious blood."

The whole principle of Calvary is the reverse
of the challenge of our text. It was for us He
died. Utterly abandoned to that divine task He
took His eyes entirely off Himself. I could weary
you with the telling of many stories where human
relationship has reached well to its highest in
tender expressions of atonement. But they are
all so feeble and incomplete when chosen as evidences of the fact our Lord has set forth in the
completeness of His Own divinity. I have read
somewhere of a wonderful creation that was
made in a workshop by a secret workman. A
young lad was employed in a shop where cathedral windows were made. It was his duty to keep
the shop in order. He picked up all the waste
and broken glass. From the shop went out many

lovely artistic windows through whose blended
beauty the attraction of great halls found new
glory. One day there was discovered and
brought forth from its hiding place, the most
wonderful window that ever came from that
workshop. Its conception was perfect. The
matchings and shadings of the tiny pieces of
which it was made were beyond compare. Ad-
mirers came from benches of design and of work-
manship to pronounce it a true masterpiece.
The patient lad had selected the broken and cast
off bits of glass and found for them their perfect
place. This great Calvary has with divine appreciation of every human experience been bringing
into significance all these fragmentary bits of
atonement out of our lives, these so often unseen
and so soon forgotten and so little appreciated
efforts of our best selves, and blending all their
meaning into one supreme effort has wrought the
unspeakably meaningful scene which set the
cross before the world forever, and made all
earth tremble as it held it up. What a message
this, to be privileged to preach to men. Sin is
such a horrible, strong, positive thing, that not
even Divinity can grapple with it and subdue it
except in strife and pain. "What pain may mean
to the Infinite and Divine; what difficulty may
mean to Omnipotence I cannot tell. Only this I
do know that all they can mean they do mean
at Calvary. Sin is never so dreadful as when

we see the Saviour with His Own blood upon His
garments. The Saviour Himself is never so dear,
never wins so utter and so tender a love as when
we see what it has cost Him to save us." Somewhat thus wrote Phillips Brooks in one of the
greatest passages to me in all the great words he
ever penned. I take my stand in absolute confidence beside the supreme fact of our faith to
read again this text of ours that the full repul-
siveness of it may be felt as the grating challenge
of unreasonable unbelief, "If Thou be the Son of
God, come down from the cross." No! No!
Thou art the Son of God! We put no "if" before
Thee. Our only hope hangs on that cross. We
would reverently bow low before the tree, and in
tears of repentance for all the sins of our lives,
which have been many, would lift our hearts to
Thee for forgiveness.

> "Weepers, come to this God,
>   For He doth weep;
> Ye sufferers come to Him.
>   For He doth care;
> Ye tremblers come,
>   For He doth mercy keep;
> Come ye who die,
>   For he doth still endure."

> "Was it for crimes that I have done,
>   He groaned upon the Tree?
> Amazing pity, grace unknown,
>   And love beyond degree."

FAITH'S ALTERNATIVE

FAITH'S ALTERNATIVE

"But if not."—*Dan. 3. 18.*

I PROPOSE from these three short, crisp, strong words, introductory to the conclusion reached by the heroic Hebrew young men before the fiery furnace, a discussion on the alternative of faith in God. All strong positions in life are faced with liability. Faith is forever threatened. These men's faith had brought them a crisis. It will always be so. Blind followers of dictated policies pitied them. Cowards bending their knees in fear before whatever asked submission, trembled for them. The king, thinking there must surely be some mistake in their persistence, had the whole matter restated to them. But they stood calm. There was no wave of emotion tossing them about, either by bold threatenings or by more careful explanation from the troubled king. They knew exactly their position, and were not troubled to know the consequences. The man who is influenced by consequences is not well grounded in conviction. Conviction that is genuine is not concerned with consequences. Pressed for an answer to the condemnation that had been declared against them they replied somewhat thus: "We, sir, are not particularly concerned to plead for your favor in this thing. If all this liability you threaten us with is true, then it will have to be. We have no concern whatever to shape our conduct to your decree whenever your decree comes in collision with our God's command. What sort of a God do you think we worship? Our God is abundantly able to deliver us out of this fiery furnace which you set for the enforcement of your decree. The only question which concerns us is, what plans He has for our particular case here now. It is no question of ability. We have God, and God can save us from that furnace if it is best so to do." Then comes this great, far-flung position of faith, the bold acceptance of all the consequences which faith must accept. They straightened themselves into the full stature of all that absolute belief in God could mean and said: "But if not! Count on that, O king. If we can escape furnaces of fire we shall surely be grateful, for genuine faith does not court suffering. But we had rather be hurled in there with faith in God, than to live and run about here among this miserable crowd of cringing cowards who will bite the dust at your every command, or any other command, just to save themselves alive. What matters it anyhow if such folks do live? We had rather die, if need be, to preserve in our souls a real conviction, than to exist without one."

This to me is one of the truly refreshing moments of all the human story. It stands easily among famous heroics. "I will trust Him though He slay me," has come singing its unfaltering triumph down many long centuries because of just such scenes. Out of lions' dens, out of furnaces of fire, out of agonies indescribable, out of choking flame and smoke on withering fagot piles, out of sorrows that swell like floods, up out of all the extreme tests that life has been able to draw against real conviction of soul, come these three mighty words of imperishable faith, "But if not."

It is my purpose now to lay emphasis upon two fundamental facts which faith must press to conclusion in all our lives.

First, there will come times to every one of us when nothing but unquestioning fidelity will keep us with God. That I count as absolute fundamental of faith. Every preacher's experience has brought him many demonstrations of that fact, wrought out in the spiritual struggles of the community to which he ministers. How easy it is for us to begin to question the dispensations of life. We put up the big word "Why?" and find ourselves so utterly unable to answer it. You cannot carry that word very far without wrecking your faith, not because your faith is poorly placed, but because your reasoning has a close horizon. I was walking one evening with one of my best friends. He had suffered a great loss, one that was far beyond repair. A loss that would not even admit of the thought of repair. He had searched in every possible direction to build him up a reasonable answer. I was trying to be like Job's friends, before they lost their balance and began to try to explain the trouble, and I was simply in silence listening to his story. He stopped suddenly, caught my shoulder and looking me in the face, said, in the finest sense of his well matured faith, "There is one thing which remains, and that is that God loves me." Right there was born the phrase I have set here as my first deduction from this alternative of faith, nothing but uncompromising fidelity can keep us with God at times. How often that fact has come glaring at us. I came home one night from a rarely beautiful and happy wedding. It was an hour when gladness was regnant and the whole occasion enforced on us all the joys of living and loving. I was glad. I came singing my way home. Life seemed good. Who couldn't love God! I had scarce entered my door, and laid off my coat when my telephone summoned me in another direction. I went out into the night. It was pitch black now. It was cold and bitter. There was no song I could hear but a moan and a sob, as I went staggering into sorrow's most awful measure. There sat a broken husband and father, with his arm around his fine young son who was sobbing on his father's breast the loss a boy so deeply realizes, and before them lay the charred fragment of wife and mother, burned to a crisp in the bitterest of accident. And out of it all came this pitiful question, "Why?" The following day I stood in a lovely home, where life has seemed to bring much of gladness. The mother came in bringing her once beautiful babe, for whose life she was now making determined battle with a frightful disease, which having been beaten off had left the little body stricken and deformed and useless, and amid the blinding tears of her very hard experience she said, "I tell you, sir, sometimes I wonder seriously over faith as I have to stand in this." And then catching herself she said, as she seemed once more to get her feet firmly under her faith again, "But I had a letter from my father only to-day and as he closed his kind words he said, 'Don't forget to trust God to the end!'" How easy it is for us, deep cut with calamity, to make unseemly inquiries into the reasons for God's ways, and to talk lightly about the failures of justice. "It is indeed quite necessary," as Samuel Johnson put it in one of those remarkable lay-sermons of his, "that our minds must be abstracted in some manner from surrounding matters if we are to be able to consider and weigh the evidences of life aright. Objects that strike us strongly to-day may do so not because they are great, but rather because they are

near, while the views of futurity may affect us but
faintly not because they are unimportant, but because they are distant." It is indeed a great day
for any life when its faith in God stands forth
strong in the fact that it is faith in God because of
God, and not because of any attendant circumstances that may seem like reward. Faith that
has not caught that issue has not caught the significance of faith at all. Nothing else is faith.
What say ye! Do you trust God here? It looks
from this close station like a mere handful of
ashes as your doom. Three men; three handfuls
of ashes. Scarce enough to cause the shaking down
of the big greedy furnace. Stop now, and consider
carefully as the first hot whiff from that withering heat there, comes chokingly into your faces.
Think well what the alternative of your faith is as
drawn against that fire there. There is the route
of your faith, your alternative lies out yonder on
cool plains beside quiet streams and laughing
careless folks who have never even thought
enough of any faith to find it in a crisis. And
the young men straightened themselves to declare
with a strength that all the ages can never
enfeeble, "Our God can save us from this burning fiery furnace, if He shall so choose. But if
not, we are utterly careless of that, for to us the
only alternative of faith is denial"—

> "It's not the fact that you're dead that counts,
> It's only—'How did you die?' "

It is said of Jesus, and I am so thankful it has been put so, that He accomplished His death. It was a part of His set task. I like to think about death that way. These young faith-daring men never once thought of whimpering at God over the matter of death. There is the presence of a grand desperation in their conduct that inspires me. They may not understand the reason of their troubles, but that never staggers their step. The path they beat on this little world here for a while is no fair horizon from which to draw conclusions against a universe, and no criterion from which to make safe judgment of the direction of eternal forces. Light alone flooding my path might blind me to a million glories I could only see from out the dark. I actually blotted from my view every star from a great glowing heaven above me one beautiful night, with my little camp-fire. I was cooking my evening meal. Such little business and such little method it was to spread across the heavens, but it did all that. I can put out every star with a crackling brush fire, and all that is no compliment to the brilliance of my blaze either. For only a short way across the bay of the little lake on whose shores I had pitched my tiny tent, I saw the twinkling light of an Indian's fire, just like mine, and it looked to me like a spark caught in the low brush along the shore, and had no effect whatever on the outstanding glories of the overbending heavens. The trouble with me was that I sat too close to the smoke and glare of my little fire, and there for me stars and constellations and whole systems, and even all the earth about me were blotted out, because I fixed my gaze upon and sat too close to my little fire. O how shall we be able to reach through immediate and personal things and learn the eternal principle of unques-tioning faith in God? He can deliver us if He so proposes; but if not——Perhaps no lesson needs learning to-day by the church more than this. So many so-called Christian faiths have been shattered on an experience that was not explain-able. Men and women have given up what they have been calling faith in God. I press the con-clusion now for an unquestioning fidelity. Faith in God will come to places in life where there will be absolutely no reason for it but just faith in God. Faith in God must sometimes be shorn of every conspiring circumstance and just left standing out stark and bare, faith in God. Often we come upon experience where all the logic of procedure is simply the genius of faith. We believe in and trust God because He is God, not because He saved us out of any fiery furnace, not because He made us rich, not because He healed our diseases, not because He did for us some little personal thing. We are in danger to-day of a modern folly which has grown up on the small idea of faith drawn out of such deliver-

ances, and which enfolds itself in strange claims
of cures for aches and pains. I am suspicious
of such selfishness calling itself faith. Who ever
made my little pain-threatened body the clearing-
house of God's justification? But I am never
suspicious of the man who can face the certain
furnace of pain and say without concern, "Burn
me if you will! But burned to a handful of
ashes though I be in body, my faith in God
remains unshaken." My faith don't stand on
what may or may not happen to me. It stands on
the fact of God. Utterly unable to sense any
path leading around the furnace, perfectly sure
the road for me leads squarely into the hot door.
I shall go on—go on, not because I can see or
cannot see, but only because I do believe. The
whole story of the Church on earth has been lit-
tered with the grave errors of those who have
sought from God something other than Himself.
So very much has the world run to God, because
men have felt they needed things primarily, and
so very often have they forgotten to pray for
God. I love to stand close to these heroic young
men of our text, who hurled all such selfishness
aside forever and branded it clearly as of no tol-
eration to faith. We do not believe because of
results. Pure faith could not be preserved with
a materialistic guarantee. Our God can deliver
us from the burning furnace. Just how, we do
not know nor care. We only know He can do it

if He chooses so to do. But if not, O king, we keep God. Sometimes, I say, in life we come to places where it requires pure desperation to save us to our faith.

The second contention I wish now to note here is, whatever is is victory for faith. Yes, I know these three heroic men came through. Their story has been told all down the ages. But there are many, many cases where suffering of the fiercest type has broken to leave never one streak of light behind it. If I am to preach to all men, and I dare not take a gospel now to preach that must have a selected hearing, I must have a faith to declare which moves upon a ground greater than earthly deliverance. There may be deliverance in store for these men, but the genius of their great declaration lies in the fact that mere deliverance was only an incident in the transaction. Our text flings deliverance as an object to the winds. Not many pass through the furnace. The furnace still must wither most of them in order to preserve the pureness of faith. There is Jeremiah. Who can find words to tell of the agony of his going? He was sawn asunder. There is John Baptist. Where has more tragic story ever been scrawled across the world's pages, aside from Calvary, than the story of the death of this great rugged man of God? I see the poor silly servant come staggering into the room, into a frivolous function of royal

society with the great bleeding head of this hero,
on a charger, the hideous prize for a dancing girl.
There's Simon Peter. We had almost lost our
patience with him at times, but at last he found
himself and stood firm in a faith that faltered
not even when they nailed him to a cross in cruel
crucifixion, head downward. There's Paul.
Great triumphant apostle brought out of the
jail, where for years he had paled his skin but
made mighty his soul, and with bent head over
the block awaiting the falling of the grinning
blade of the axeman, shouting a triumph the
world was sure to hear. There go Polycarp
and Savonarola and Latimer and Huss and Rid-
ley, and O, an army, an army of them, going up
to heaven on wings of smoke and fire. There is
Jesus Christ, Son of God, Lover of mankind,
mobbed on the wild street of a mad town. Spit
upon, scourged, beaten, mocked, nailed to a cross.
My God! My God! has He been forsaken! Dead
on the cross. Dead before His hating, triumphant persecutors. Dead! Jesus Christ dead! O
yes, I know God can deliver us, "But if not."

Some captains of some badly battered ships
that came limping into port one day, after the
worst storm I have ever seen had swept the seas
to an accumulated fury of three days and nights,
told me that there were times when the storm
was so bad that all they could do was to stay at
sea, to put straight back into the teeth of the

gale. My father used to sing much about
our home that old song, simple, but perhaps
more beautiful now to me for its simplicity,
"Jesus loves me, this I know, for the Bible tells
me so." I can hear the note of his song through
all the years, and he sang to the last. He has
sung it into my soul. I always keep that point
clear. Whenever I become fearful at my visions,
I turn again and sing it over, "Jesus loves me,
this I know." Keep right on, O trembling heart.
Try that calm trust to-day. When James Guthrie
walked forth to the scaffold to give up his life
rather than his faith, he said in answer to a prof-
fered deliverance, "I durst not redeem my life
with the loss of my integrity." He struck again
the great note of victory. Can you? Can I? My
God is able to deliver me, but if not! The only
alternative of faith is denial.

IMPERFECTION'S PROPHECY

IMPERFECTION'S PROPHECY

"I shall be satisfied, when I awake, with thy likeness."—
Psa. 17. 15.

THAT is a bold ideal for a man to announce. It
seems to be flavored with audacity as it looks up
and away from the consciousness of mortality
and dares to express a dissatisfaction anywhere
this side of divine likeness. Yet with all its
audacity I confess to a fondness for it, because
of its upreach. I am really glad to hear man
stand out bold to his bigness, and state that
nothing short of the highest will suit his ideal.
I am very sure that this restlessness in ideal is
one of his chief credentials. Someone has defined
man as "a becoming." The more that short definition is thought through, the more its fitness
will appear. All the history of his life and hopes,
and the heaping evidence of his unfailing death,
bring to our minds the truth of this upward
struggle. How empty-handed he falls always.
How utterly bare does death shake his hands.
How unsatisfied after all, he makes his toilsome
way about his little world. He is forever in
pursuit of pleasure, and never satisfied that he
has found it. There seems no measure to his
capacity. Carlyle declares in one of the most

wonderful chapters in modern literature, that
"all the finance ministers, upholsterers and con-
fectioners of modern Europe could not undertake
in joint stock company to make one shoe-black
happy. If they did it, they could not hold it
above an hour, and that brief time only as a
delusion. For the shoe-black also has a soul
quite as much as a stomach, and he would
require, if you consider it for his permanent satisfaction and saturation simply this allotment,
no less and no more! God's infinite universe all
to himself, therein to enjoy infinitely and fill
every wish as fast as it arose. Try him with
half a universe of an omnipotence, and he sets
quarreling with the proprietor of the other half.
Always there is a black spot in our sunshine. It
is simply that persistent shadow of ourselves."
Now I do not know what there was to tempt the
shoe-black of the day when Carlyle wrote thus.
But this I do know, there never were more dissatisfied children on earth than those of to-day
into whose laps have fallen such gifts as no other
childhood ever knew.

> "A jumping-jack and a candy-stick,
>   A doll and a ribbon bow,
> These made the hearts of the children beat quick
>   A hundred years ago."

But the child of to-day cannot be so easily
pleased. I saw a toy sail-boat in a show window the other day, marked in bold confident fig-

ures at fifty dollars. It has ere this been taken
home for some boy to set sail in a pond, and throw
well placed rocks at to aid a slow breeze or assist
a poor working rudder to guide. With a fifty
dollar boat there will be no more satisfaction had,
than with the one I had, whittled out of a picked-
up board, and rigged with a piece of my mother's
cast off apron. I am saying to you in these boy
terms, a fact that runs in never tiring significance through all human life. There is something within us which looks ahead, and dares to
set its satisfaction in the safe fastnesses of God-
likeness. To my way of thinking, this persistent
dissatisfaction is a great prophet, and herein is
found one of the richest and most undeniable
arguments of faith. "I shall be satisfied, when I
awake in His likeness." What is the meaning of
this far-reaching sense of incompleteness? Why
am I so everywhere dissatisfied? Why weary myself digging down the mountains nature piled?
Why forever tunneling a new route through
seemingly misplaced hills? Why dredge out
huge canals, and pour two oceans together at
Panama? Why seek to improve my continent-
locked lakes, and link them to the ocean to dock
my ships mid-continent from a world's harbors?
What ails this man, set to live a short mortal life
upon so interesting a world as is this, that he
cannot be satisfied with it as it is, and yet, never
has been able to build it into a condition that

came any nearer satisfaction than it was before?
Man forever outruns his home. He is forever
ahead of the world. He is too big to be mortal.

What does all this mean anyhow, or does it
men anything more than mad confusion? Does
it merely shame us with assured destruction, or
does it spur us with a sure continuance to-morrow? The fact is we are conscious of imperfection. No man has ever yet been able to look
forward and think out an accepted perfection.
The perfections aspired to yesterday are the
unsatisfactory possessions of to-day. Each attain-
ment we make leads to a new lifted ideal. There
is a tireless leadership in perfection which lures
us a step at a time, but forever lures us. Men
were early content with small ambitions toward
close lying possessions. They pressed into wider
fields only as they occupied those close joining.
They ventured out upon unknown oceans only as
they chafed at the well-paced bounds of conti-
nents. The savage who roamed this splendid wilderness and found his wild living in the forests
and streams, had no ambition to dock his boats
in distant cities across an ocean. Emerson has
somewhere a passage something thus. I do not
quote him exact but the meaning is all his. There
is a perfect chain of reforms emerging from the
darkness. Every aggressive movement of mankind bears evidence of the great general idea.
The history of reform is always the same, it

springs forever from the comparison of the idea
with the fact. We arraign our daily employments. They are unfit, unworthy the faculties
we spend on them. When we converse with a
wise man we find ourselves apologizing for our
employments. We speak of them with shame.
It is a shame born at the low altars of a life
unworthy our higher consciousness, shame therefore the herald of our finest nature. Out of this
fair ideal of the mind, springs the ambition for
and the effort toward the perfect. It is the in-
terior testimony to a fairer possibility of life
which forever agitates society with the offer of
some new amendment. There is a fond statement
Schopenhauer used to make about a man never
able to be happy because he of necessity being
some one thing, still has within him the idea
and desire of being a thousand other things.
Every poverty we endure is haunted with the
idea of the riches that would vanish it. In fact
that is exactly what poverty is. Poverty is not
merely the absence of cash. The beast of the
field has no cash, yet poverty is not his word.
If you object to the comparison I will take the
old Indian I met far in the north woods. He
had no money. I could have bought half a canoe
full of blue-berries for a dollar. Yet the conception of poverty as we know it down the alleys of
our cities was no word for him. He had a forest
about him. Moose and deer and grouse and fish

and berries and nuts and bark were there. Poverty is that haunting ghost that points to rags and empty larder in contrast to what others have to enjoy. It was a rare old Connecticut character who was buried in a quiet little churchyard, and had raised over him a simple little stone on which were these strong words, "Here lies a rich man, whose riches consisted in the fewness of his wants." How rich a man could be to-day if he could but reduce his wants to a few. But we are living with a multiplied list of wants. Our poverty seems to consist in the multitude of our wants. Everything we have is haunted by a contrast of a better possession of some other. Decrepitude muses on youth. An old man, hobbling his slow but thoughtful way along our walk the other day, stopped me as I stepped off the walk to go pounding ahead of him in my rush. He stuck out his cane and said, "Hold on, young fellow! When you get as old as I be, you won't run by like that." And I stopped a while to set my pace to his slow step long enough to say, "Old man, you are right. I know it as well as you do; and if I had the time now I would welcome the privilege of walking with you. But just at this period I must hurry." And I went quickly on, leaving him falling farther and farther behind now. What a world this is? I called to a patient plow-boy one day I saw turning the end of his furrow to start back across a long field, and asked him what he was thinking about. You might think it was how to set the plow to cut the furrow, or how long till evening, or how far it was across the field, but he answered me quickly, "I was thinking of my big office in the great city some day." The possible and the unrealized in every life need attention. These faculties which we set to work every morning at our desks or benches or counters, with which we make what we call our living, are only a very small part of our strength. We are set so much at small things. Nine parts of our real selves seem to lie idle. The sense of imperfection strews the human path everywhere. It has written its story in the huge waste piles of progress. The junk-pile is not all failure. The size of the junk-pile is compliment to the age. You might reckon it as a sure register of the speed of progress. We are plunging forward now at wild rate. Rag-pickers, scrap-iron gatherers, junk pilers, are an army among us. Red-rusted machinery flung in great heaps on every side. Engines, wagons, automobiles, trucks, lathes, ranges, rails, bolts, buttons, bars, pins. A veritable mountain of stragglers who could not keep up with the march. Someone once said, "The Yankee leads the world because he is not afraid of a junk-pile." He don't wear things out. He passes them, and they lose their use to him. All this is but a glaring illustration of one of the most profound facts of life.

It is worth our while to look imperfection, or our consciousness of imperfection, square in the face, and matching that consciousness against our aspiration for perfection, seek an explanation. Such a glaring fact as this, written across this world's material as well as spiritual life, is not without meaning. Man has set himself with wonderful patience and design to evolve the crude things he has found on this world into a better conception he has framed for them. He thinks at times it is an innate pessimism within him that suggests that he could have made a better world himself, until his optimism answers with the declaration that that is exactly what we are doing here. The wild-crab which grew to a mere knot of bitterness on the twig of a wild tree, offered the opportunity for a care and improvement which brought at last a "Brother Jonathan" or one that an enthusiast has dared name "Seek no Further." Man criticized the simple petaled wild-rose, and attacking its simplicity with soil and climate and selection evolved a wonder on a green stem and called it an "American Beauty." This innate pessimist chafed at the simple faced daisy which blew its possibilities in his fields, and with studious care he curled every petal, and multiplied every component of its yellow throat into a perfect tangle of beauty which he calls a chrysanthemum. He changes the modest ring-dove into the strange shapes the pigeon-fanciers covet. He evolves a yellow despised cur, until he mounts in favor from the alleys to which he was born to the soft cushions of lovely limousines. Take the hand of ambitious, aspiring man off this world and it would slink back again to its basal position of wild-crabs and wild-roses and wild-daisies and wilderness. Is there any testimony to be had from all these imperfections on which designing purpose will win such great results? I am thoroughly convinced that "the crooked lines of nature are the master strokes of God." There was a day when blundering atheism tried to use all this as argument against God. But they reasoned with too short a perspective. Perturbations indicate more perfect lines of action, and when man can trail the inconsistencies, which he calls perturbations in a planet's orbit, across the heavens and determine from that planet's faltering and failures to keep perfect time as scheduled in this man's studio, and on the trail of such detected imperfection can reach out into unknown space and find a hitherto unknown planet, thus discovering Neptune, man gives me there a figure of his endless struggle on the trail toward perfection. His recognized imperfections are the blazes on his infinite pathway.

Let us turn now to face this fact in the realm of our highest nature. Upon every hand our imperfections lie. We catalogue them thus, sick-

ness, failure, pain, privation, bereavement, and
many familiar more. Can we find any argument
here? It is possible for us to live with hardships
until we become unconscious of them. There
lies within four blocks of this pulpit, a fine old
character who has suffered on as painful a bed
as any man was ever wracked upon, for eight
long years now. He lies a drawn victim of disease. Pain is in every joint. His body is tortured all out of shape. One eye went out some
time since, with a pain that almost took his life.
I went in to see him recently. I had not seen
him for a few weeks, and the dear old man smiled
at me and lifted up his pain-knotted fist which
I dared not take in my hand, no matter how ten-
derly, and the tears ran down his old drawn face
for his wife to wipe from pain-graven cheek. I
said, "How are you to-day?" And out of all
these things I have been telling you he answered
me, "O, my digestion is bothering me a little
to-day, but otherwise I am feeling about as
usual." I am saying that we can actually go to
bed with much of the world's suffering until it
becomes commonplace. "Therefore, my beloved
brethren, be ye steadfast, unmovable, always
abounding in the work of the Lord, forasmuch
as ye know your labor is not in vain in the Lord,"
and "you shall be satisfied when you awake in
His likeness." That, after all, is the underlying
secret of your dissatisfaction. Nothing less will

satisfy you. The scourging of imperfection is the whip-cord that drives men and women on to truth. You are ashamed of your failure, it is the argument of your higher relationship.

We are forever conscious of our shortcomings, not that we did not aspire nobly, but that we forever fell short. We are so wont to make a footing of results in the lives we know. I am oft called to bury the body of some one who has struggled for years merely to keep a pulse going. I said the last words one difficult day over the pale, frayed-out body of a man whose whole effort for fourteen years had been to keep alive, only to be made an object of torture living. For ten years before he took sick, he had spent all the strength he had away from the sheer task of making a living, at nursing the tortured body of a wife who was on the closest terms with all that mortal suffering means. What a contradiction that, simply keeping alive. Each day to merely choke down enough nourishment to feed exist- ence. Such imperfection is astounding. That man had aspirations. His soul saw visions. His heart leaped to ambition. He was an iron- molder. In his line he had been an expert. There he lay for years unable even to lift a hand, and the world wanted iron. See the contradiction. For years he must withdraw himself from all ministry of helpfulness though naturally im- pelled thereto. In order to live at all, he must do nothing but merely live. That's not human life. Could we measure what he actually was, beside what he aspired to be we would say, here was a man who utterly failed. I count it real joy to face so trying a fact of imperfection with the good news of Christianity. I would say beside every hard pressed soul, and over every grave where sleep the remains of those who fell before their victory was in any way manifest on this earth, "Your labor is not in vain in the Lord, for Christ hath brought immortality to light." Life does not consist merely of that which we see stumbling about this dark earth for a few brief years, feeling its way along flinted paths, worn to collapse with hard work, and snuffed out at last like a candle. Every cry of our hearts is for a fair chance. I have just come back from the grave of a tiny babe, every breath of whose short stay here was drawn in pain, and aside from awakening the rich sense of parentage in two fine young lovers here, that babe did nothing more on this earth. We posted in our church bulletin only recently the name of as fine and manly a young man as our record held. He had just bloomed into strong manhood and was ready. He had won his wings in war and had begun in business clean and strong. Accident struck him down and he fell into the deep, deep grave of youth. This very week gone I went with the sisters of a big strong man in his youth, to lay

his body away after recovery from our river
where he drowned. He had crossed the ocean
twenty times in the perils of war, and in the
exposed storms of a winter swept north route,
and came home to founder to his death on our
quiet river in days of peace. But all this is but
the regular diary out of my ministry just now, it
runs on through the years thus. If life is what
it seems, it is surely largely a failure, and I am
not surprised to see the pathetic emblems used
in our grave-yards, the broken columns, quenched
torches, and closed urns. Imperfection is glaring. Contradiction confounds us. I would make
bold to step into just such a condition with the
message of the Gospel. Christianity does not
deny these things, nor does it seek to avoid
them. It has a message for them. It is not a
message of Nirvana, the hope of annihilation. It
is the promise of deliverance. Christianity
gathers argument in life's imperfections and
proposes heaven's perfection. It hangs before
our conscious failures the available victories in
Jesus Christ, and declares that the very fact that
we call so much of life imperfect is an argument
that we are set for better things. How can we
draw a standard of imperfection unless there be
in our ideals the higher standard of perfection?
Jesus Christ stands at the breakdown of our
ideals, and offers us eternal life in which we
can pursue perfection. Take courage, thou suf-

fering stricken soul. It takes the hot forges of
death itself to weld to you the glory of the great
to-morrow. Green, the great English historian,
cried in pathetic voice as death choked him down,
"I have so much work to do." Cecil Rhodes, than
whom no more colossal worker was produced by
the nineteenth century, when compelled to lay
down life at less than fifty years of age, just
when his plans seemed to need him most, cried
out as he fell, "So much to do, so little done."
That thrilling explorer of the antarctic region,
Scott, who died in the desolations of the deserts
of ice and snow, went staggering on to the very
last dragging step and died crying, "Slog on!
Slog on! Slog on!" How convincingly eloquent
all this! Man's efforts are forever falling short
of his own ambitious possibility. Don't you
detect that peculiar cry for perfection ringing
through all these imperfections? Immortality
in my judgment is foretokened most eloquently
in such seeming discrepancies. The very fact
that we feel life falter, is argument of some
higher ideal from which it has faltered. At the
very best here on earth we only work away at the
bare directions of our destiny. We do well if
we even get the pillars of our temple so much
as blocked out, if we even set the chisels of our
purpose in the hard rock of privilege enough to
mark out the outlines of our higher ambitions.
There is convincing evidence of wisdom written

in all this incompleteness. Someone has said, I
believe it was Bushnell, though I could not turn
to it, that "We could not be successfully trained
for immortality in a time element that was in
itself just as good and as reliable as immortality.
It must not be as good and reliable or we would
plan to remain in it." If we are to rise to something higher we must see clearly the unreliable,
imperfect things about us, and under the guid-
ance of such a fact must leap to the higher and
better things for which our hungry hearts have
always throbbed. This is the philosophy of the
imperfect, the prophecy of the incomplete. Only
man is unfinished. Only man chafes under the
consciousness of a perfection forever above him.
I arise this hour to say, out of such history as we
have been noting, and sure of no satisfaction
being found anywhere this side, "I shall be satisfied when I awake in His likeness." Till that
day dawns, I shall take my dissatisfaction as my
prophet and listen ever to his voice and go forward.

THUS FAR, SAFE

THUS FAR, SAFE

THUS FAR, SAFE

"When the Son of man cometh, shall he find faith on the earth?"—*Luke 18: 8.*

"I have kept the faith."—*2 Tim. 4: 7.*

THIS question of Jesus Christ, which is a concluding word at the close of a short parable contending that "men ought always to pray and not to faint," is one of the strangest words to me to be found in the Bible. It is introduced with the word "nevertheless." It seems to be a full intended question He asked, after endeavoring to tell them an essential thing they should do, and then realizing that so much preaching fails to move to action, He challenges them thus, "Nevertheless, when the Son of Man cometh shall He find faith in the earth?" He lifted His eyes to look away, down the centuries, and press for answer amid all the life of a very troubled world could mean; will faith languish and droop, and decay and finally die out of this world I came to redeem? When I come again, will My reception be as cold and cruel and heartless as the one these Jews have given Me now? This is one of the strangest words in the Bible. I shall not endeavor to explain it, but I do want to make bold to answer it just as it is asked, and upon

73

the fine word of Paul as he stood triumphant as
far as he could go in this world, I want once
more to lift an answer out of this hour. In the
midst of one of the greatest crises the world
has ever had to meet, it is altogether becoming
of Christianity to be asking itself this question
now. What is the status of the faith? What is
Christianity doing? What is uppermost in human attention now, things secular that are passing away, or things spiritual and abiding?

We have heard much about the failure of
Christianity. It was a favorite note upon which
a persistent pessimism piped all through the war,
the echoes of which have not yet died. Many
men who had set themselves to the performance
of some little programs, and had failed to find
the assistance they expected, have been sure in
drawing the failing conclusion. It is hard not
to see the collapse of everything when your own
little something goes down. Men frequently look
out from under the wreck of their little ceilings
and imagine the heavens have fallen. I shall
make bold now to match against that keen
pointed question of Christ, which I am sure
should put the edge of responsibility in personal
manner to all our hearts, this very personal declaration from Paul, a man in whom religion was
a life of ever growing power. I seek to find an
answer for my Lord as a personal conclusion,
and to talk now to the personal responsibility in

us all for the keeping of the faith. For after all, as to me myself, it is of no consequence whatever in molding my action toward the faith of my own heart if every other one on earth should fail, my business is to keep the faith myself. I am not in it because it is a popular movement. I shall not find reason to desert it because it may become unpopular. My confidence does not found itself upon a crowd that stands with me, nor does my fear arise from a crowd that is against me. My faith is in God solely for God's sake. I want always to enter into my duties toward my faith with the overwhelming sense of my personal responsibility.

> "Stand fast to your faith!
> It shall live through the years,
> And sustain you through tears.
> It shall teach you to smile,
> Though the whole world revile;
> To the dark cruel end
> It shall serve as your friend,
> It shall help you to bear
> Every burden of care.
> Stand fast to your faith!"

I heard a young lady giving her testimony in a meeting the other night say, "I want to work as though there were no God, and I want to pray as though there were none else." O if we could but sweep clean the sky of our duty, and behold ourselves standing stark and alone, responsible for the issue. Work, as though there were none other. Our hearts bound to be strong. Our hands bound to be potent. Every time I read this pathetic question of Christ's, "When I come again, shall I find faith in the earth?" I always like to turn right to this fine triumphant word of the most militant and soul-stirring disciple Christianity has yet produced, and answer it at least that far down the ages, and then in a significant personal sense fling it on down the toiling centuries, as millions more have found it to word their own confident experiences, and gather confidence thus, even down to this very hour, "I have kept the faith." O I can hear it all the way. Just as long as our religion is able to lead the individual soul all the way and usher it out of this world with this note on its lips, it will be secure here. I heard one of America's greatest preachers declare himself in a most impressive manner at a convention of Christian men in Atlantic City one day. We were discussing the program of the church for reconstruction days. We were talking about all the ordinary problems that so easily monopolize about all our conferences and conventions. This preacher arose and said in most convincing manner something like this: "Brethren, I am interested in all this discussion, and I believe in the purpose of it all. But I have come here right from the bedside of one of my dearest friends who is sick unto certain death. The last thing I did before I left home

was to tell him good-bye, and to look into his
fading eyes. He has been one of the leading business men in my city, a constructive force in righteousness. He has been a man of profound interest in all the big social programs. He has been
a reformer in every good cause. But just now
there is not to him any interest in all that. He
is right where he wants to know, what of it if
we are reformed? He don't want a social message, he wants a personal message, and he said,
as he held my hand to tell me good-bye and bid
me God-speed down here, not expecting to be
alive to welcome me home again, 'Tell those men
down there for me that we want a certain message for the time when we have to step off this
world and leave.' " As Dr. Johnston Myers dared
to drop that pertinent note, which seemed at once
to be almost on a tangent to our consideration, it
brought keenly to all our hearts the fact that after
all the prime question ever before us is keeping
the faith. I, even I can keep the faith. Then,
my Lord, I would stand square up to this difficult day of ours when the keeping of the faith
means so very much, and promise you I will keep
it. I would rejoice to see the faith regnant in
this world's life. But whatever any, or every
other one may do, I propose to be faithful. Just
how far this side my completed testimony I am
now I cannot tell, but my determination I would
measure by the standard of a testimony offered

in our Prayer Meeting recently by a splendid
Christian man who said, "I have been a Christian now for sixteen years, and if I knew when
I was going to die I could tell you exactly how
much longer I am going to be a Christian in this
world." The colored folks used to sing a quaint,
and yet in its utter simplicity a very impressive
hymn called The Old Time Religion. "It was
good enough for Moses. It was good enough for
Daniel. It was good for Paul and Silas. It
was good enough for father. It was good enough
for mother. It is good enough for me." And one
great triumphant day I want to come to the hour
where I can register the close of my earthly
career in these same great words, "I have kept
the faith." If You come now, Lord, You will find
the faith in the earth! He who keeps the faith
shall find at last that the faith has kept him. His
preservation will only come as he guards his
trust, and may come only as the price of his
extreme devotion.

> "The kings of eternal evil
> Still darken the hills about;
> Thy part is, with broken saber,
> To rise on the last redoubt,
> To fear no sensible failure,
> Nor covet the game at all,
> But fighting, fighting, fighting,
> Die! Driven against the wall."

That was what Paul meant, and that was exactly what he did. You hear no other note from

him. Never a whimper from him. Never an uncertain word. No negotiation for compromise. Everywhere this same note. He never lost his posture. Timidity about ultimate issues never disturbed him. He was an ultimate issue himself. He fought and labored in the spirit of certain triumph. He was no blind fanatic. He was not a stranger to opposition. And after such an uncompromising life he met death in a manner that has kept him a living example across the ages. One day I walked down the wheel-worn pavements of Pompeii. The memories of the ancient city haunted every corner of the ruins, and seemed to leap out from every street, and scurry across the Forum and over the Arena, their once famous play-house. But amid it all nothing has come to me with such impress as the story of that famous Roman soldier whose faithfulness has stood down all the buried centuries, and compels now the appreciation of every visitor who stands at the corner where he was told to stand so long ago. They found him standing there. Standing! His spear still in hand. Unmoved, while the very mouth of hell opened wide to pour destruction over the city. unmoved, while the terrified thousands were clamoring down the choking streets, and fleeing to the hills, falling in the stifling smoke, crawling a little farther there to die. While the earth reeled and staggered like a drunken man, that soldier stood at his post of duty. And the first word that leaped from the lips of the men who found him standing there eighteen centuries later, the word that unmoved man has driven into the heart of the whole world even with his dead hands, dead all these centuries, was "true to his trust." They have picked up many bodies there. "They find them prostrate and marked with torture and pain. They found one woman at the city's outer gates, fallen, clutching in her determined hands her treasured jewels." That crowd was running. Had the soldier joined them he too would have been but one more discovery of the mere victims of mad destruction. But he fled not, and when the world found him they heard his message across the years.

I sometimes go walking with my library, back across the long centuries just to get their encouraging words. Back through persecution and suffering and martrydom. Back through battles, and dungeons, and fagot-piles, and crucifixions. "I have kept the faith," comes forever out of them. Sometimes gurgled through the strangling waters as the tides of the Solway at Sterling bore away the spirit of Margaret Wilson and left her body tied to the stake there. Sometimes breathing out of the scorching flames in the famous square at Florence where Savonarola leaped out to world-power. This triumphant answer to Christ's challenging question has come down all the years. I gather confidence in that fact this hour. It is the power of genuine religious experience. If Paul could keep the faith, who am I, that I should dare face the end of my journey with any less equipment? I will keep the faith. It must be a joy in heaven to record down the years the full triumphs of the faithful. Many good, triumphant souls, whose names are not known off their own humble streets on this earth, but down to the last breath bring life triumphant and lay it clean at the feet of Jesus. These are the answers to my Lord. There are thousands, yea, millions of these keepers of the faith in this hard pressed old world of ours to-day. Patient, tried, tempted, troubled, but unfaltering men and women. Often the fiercest fight they have to make is that they must go on unnoticed and alone. But virtue when watched is not to be compared to virtue which knows no one can see. One day came to me a wrinkled, soiled page, written in great suffering. The pain of every pen-stroke stood clear in that writing. It said this, "I am dying, and from the edge of my grave I send you this greeting in assurance of the salvation which glows bright in my soul. I want you to preach my funeral sermon. Yours in the Faith, Mrs. John Rooney." That brief note meant more to me than to any other. She was the first soul my all too barren ministry ever won to the Kingdom. I shall never forget the night I saw her

arise from the back seat of that little country
church, and walk down that aisle and kneel at
the altar. She was a humble little woman, living in a little farm-cottage, off the main-road and
known to very few. She never did become known
to many, but she kept the faith. And when a hungry old cancer found her out there, lonely, and
without many friends, and set at its mean work
to eat her life out, she might have let her faith
go and made little difference to the church, you
may say. But she didn't, and she died in glorious
victory, and once more dated the declaration
Jesus has been listening for down the ages. It
has not been a great many years since I first began to preach this great faith with that sincere
confidence and enthusiasm of a young preacher,
who not knowing much of what life really meant,
went forth unquestioningly to declare victory.
For something over twenty-five years now I have
been trying to preach, and year by year have I
been gathering confirming evidence of my faith.
The more I have preached, the more the accumulated evidence of the worth of the Christian message has impressed me. To-day it means so much
more than it could have meant to me when I
went new to my first charge and arose in a little
country pulpit to speak my faith. Most precious
memories come now crowding about to testify.
Then I had only my own experience to stand on.
But now I have the confirming testimonies of

many I have sat beside, and heard them again and
again down the years call out these words of Paul,
as death reached for them, "I have kept the faith!"
Thus far it is safe, Lord! I have seen the faith
spring anew in hearts that had seemed to let it
die. I have seen God forgive the faithless one,
and start him once more on virtue's path. I have
come to know how slow to anger and how plen-
teous in mercy He is. And to-day there is not
one phase of the faith that I have not been privileged to see hold in the sweeping flood of great
waters. The simple mention of these incidents
I have been calling here, will but stir in the memories of all who see these words, to the multiplied
more you know in confirming testimony. Thank
God the faith about which our Lord inquired is
safe thus far. The faith we have to-day is not a
mere trust in a dogma. It is not a mere agree-
ment to a set of declarations which we repeat in
simple memory. The faith which Paul kept, and
which he handed up in testimonial answer to his
Lord ere the axeman struck his noble head from
his bent shoulders; the only faith any man can
keep, or that is worth the keeping of any man, is
the one that sustains him. A faith that proves
itself peculiarly his in the shock of great trial.
A faith unusually bright and glorious when the
scourge was falling with fierce hissing across
his naked bleeding back in the jail at Philippi. A
faith peculiarly precious when the mad mob

shook their clenched fists at him, and clamored
for his blood about the staircase of the Judgment
Hall in Jerusalem. A faith that triumphantly
held up his clanking chains before the trembling
Judge, before whom he came staggering and
emaciated from the stagnant prison where he had
been waiting for two fierce years, all because of
his confidence in God. A faith that could there
shake the mocking shackles of such imprisonment before his listeners, and enlist his cause
there with boldest appeal. A faith that stood
calm when the storm-tossed ship shivered on the
flinted teeth of Malta, and waded ashore to calm
deliverance. A faith that walked in triumph,
though bound in chains, down Roman streets,
and sat down again amid stifling imprisonment
to make forever famous Mamertine there. A
faith that flung encouragement back to the world
from that dungeon darkness, defied the block,
and sang the victor's song to the headsman as
his noble head fell. I have kept the faith! I
have kept the faith. And poor, humble, unworthy preacher of such a faith that I am, I
nevertheless feel a defiance with it now, and feel
a confidence that allows me to say that a faith
like that will keep me too. I would lift my
voice amid the crash and roar and materialistic
emphasis the world is hearing these Twentieth
Century days of ours, to plead with every one of
you for a place in your hearts for this grand old

faith. We have a faith that has had shed upon
it more of the greatest experience of the human
soul than can ever be measured. It has been
wrought out of the very heart of God Himself,
and endorsed with the blood of Jesus Christ His
Son. About that faith and upon it, has been
wrought out by all these years of experience, by
successes and reverses, by joys and by sorrows, a
whole human circle of testimony. It is a faith
upon which everything that is worth while has
been risked, that no man or woman can afford
to be without, and that no soul under any condition can afford to surrender. I would God now,
that I could snatch up this great strain across
the ages, and waft it up to the Throne from this
great day of ours, and from the very heart of all
our strenuous endeavors shout to the waiting
ears of heaven, "We have kept the faith!" God
forgive us that we have done so very little for
it, and with it among men, but we have at least
kept it alive. We should now press the conflict
and make it triumphant.

How superior to all his experiences, and how
needless of any of our pity, is the soul who walks
out the span of experience with unfaltering faith
in God, accepts all struggle and hardship as mere
incidents of the road, and wraps himself up in
the mastering safety of a faith that knows no
timidity, but presses ever onward, bearing always
upon his face the beams of an unfailing triumph

to-morrow, and at last as the shimmering rays
of eternal life stream in at the eastern window,
leaves his final word, "I have fought a good fight,
I have finished my course, I have kept the faith."
O let us register it firmly as our purpose now.
Come now and join me in the name of the fought-
out-to-the-end issue in us all.   Let us strike hands
in unquenchable faith in our Master now.   O
God! I cry for myself, count me.   Just now in
the thick of the fight of manhood at noontime!
Now, when the tang of temptation can drive its
sharpest bolt into my soul!   Now, when if I
should falter or fail it would be calamity of
treachery in the very battle's line!   Right now,
Lord, I lift my hand to register my allegiance,
I swear my eternal loyalty, and at last, by Thy
good grace, I will see to it that it shall be sealed
with my very last breath here on earth, whenso-
ever that hour shall come.   I propose to keep
the faith—I will

> "Charge again then and be dumb;
> Let the victors when they come,
> And the forts of folly fall,
> Find my body by the wall,"

and draw back and say, "He kept the faith!"

DEFIANT FAITH

DEFIANT FAITH

"I can do all things through Christ which strengtheneth me."—*Phil. 4. 13.*

THAT word is bold, to fanaticism. It leaves no way for escape in its judgment. It contains no qualifying clause. It leaps out in bold defiance, assured of God. When once we have committed our case to a statement so clear, and likewise so extreme, men have not only the right, but the immediate inclination to conclude that here is either fanaticism or fact. Paul is in line here with Christianity which must forever prove itself against even the impossible, or rank as fanaticism. Christianity faces directly the alternative that it is either of God or is the boldest hypocrisy. It has been everywhere, through its most expressive characters, and by its frank teachings, creating this dilemma. It has not done it in ignorance, nor does the fact bring fear to its cause. The boldness of this text is an outstanding example. Paul, even then a prisoner in bonds, an unknown Jew, a persecuted preacher, a poor tent-maker from Tarsus, speaks up amid such contradicting facts as these, and declares, "I can do all things," and his prison-keepers must have laughed as they knew the

chains he couldn't break, and the great overwhelming city of Rome whose prison he must
languish in. "Who is this Lilliputian spokes-
man who seems to know so little of what 'all
things' means, or else talks utterly at random!"
And that is just why I choose now this word
for a text. It draws the religious issue squarely.
Such a word is either an utterly idle song or a
tremendous fact. If it be an idle song, we will
dismiss the speaker as another of the many fanatics religion has developed. If it be a com-
manding fact, we will have struck the path of
God among men.

One time in preaching from that familiar appeal of Jesus, "Come unto me, all ye that labor,
and I will give you rest," I said, "The one who
uttered that was either crazy or divine, and
Christianity is willing for the judgment." I say
now, before this bold word of Paul, that has
come on down an exposure of almost two thousand years of the most scrutinizing research mankind has ever known; years that have left in
their ruck the claims and professions of millions
of fanatics and impostors in religion; I say as
one who is at least in search of truth wherever it
can be found among men, that the crisis which
Paul drew upon our faith with these words, was
not the boast of an idle fanatic, but rather the
frank declaration of a genuine faith in God. I
eagerly seek to get myself up beside such a

speaker, and accept with the same faith in the
same God the same alternative of position, and
while such an unlimited contract makes me feel
personally the keen limitations of my own ability,
that is perhaps religion's first essential, for it
savors the more of God. Our efforts have often
failed because we have tried to get on with too
little of God. While that is the empowerment of
it all, it is likewise the safe governor of it all.
It is a dangerous thing to grant to a man unlimited power, "All things," it says here. That
scares me. If that be humanly true, I have
nothing but dread of him who wields so mighty
an arm. If it be possible I would dread to be
endowed with it. Its liability humbles me with
responsibility. You must remember the anxiety
which was throughout England over the careless
conduct of Edward, Prince of Wales. But the
first breath of the responsibility imposed upon
him by his coronation sobered him into a gracious
king. "I can do all things." Is that the boast of
an ambitious man? Then I shall shun him. But
the limitation, and the qualification which keeps
this forever the safe fact of genuine religion is
the condition, "through Christ," for that partnership can only be had in things of His Own
Spirit.

The thing that is interesting me just now
before such a word, and before such a world as
this, where so much remains yet to be done, and

where we have so hard a time to persuade folks
to understake this partnership with divinity in
program, is the fact that the church stands to-day
throughout almost the whole world with its declared aims and purposes yet unfulfilled, and yet
committed to the fact Paul uncompromisingly
announced. Some will say it is not diplomatic.
It leaves no way of escape. There is no available ground for compromise. There is much that
is not yet done. There are many of us who have
done very little. What ails these folks who
call themselves Christians, and link themselves
up to so pretentious a program, and yet after so
many years witness on every hand the falterings
of their endeavors? Surely there is nothing in
all the world's story that needs attention more
than the things to which our religion is directed.
We stand committed. If we can do these things,
we had better be busying ourselves upon them,
for I wonder often just how far divine patience
will wait upon us, who square before the need
of the religion, and a sorrow-filled world because
that religion is not in complete sway there, spend
ourselves and our talents upon the small things
which cluster themselves around our pleasures.
When once I allow such a thought to catch my
attention I feel as though I never again would
care to spend an ounce of my poor little strength
in any other direction than directly to the goal
of my faith. I read the story of China, and it

breaks my heart with need. India, Africa, Mexico, South America, America's cities, O God, give me some sort of a life that may make contact for Thy great saving Gospel in every place I may live among men.

Providence presents many very pertinent questions to all our minds. Many men, bothered in explaining the operations of life inside the short-tethered experience they call their own, would make the universe a mere chance-medley. There are many, who to-day are trying to hide their lack of religion behind the small plea that they could not hold out. Men have learned little how to measure their access to God. The sum total of the strength of a man they would measure as in his arm and brain. While there are some achievements which make man proud as he contemplates what he has done, some noble architecture, some world-embracing invention, yet mankind as a whole, as well as individually, has had enough experience to recognize the hard fact that in some places we might seem to succeed, but in others we are bound to lose, and at the end we come stumbling or creeping up to a lowly grave to rest our worn-out mortality, whether it be the Sage of Skibo, lately laid to rest in Sleepy Hollow, after amassing millions of money, and writing his name in granite across the threshold of a thousand structures round the world, or whether it be the marbled form of infancy that

never came to consciousness beyond the circle of
its mother's breast. Life is often a conflict of
consciousness, a pitched battle between my
strength and my weakness. There do come times
of triumph to me. But times of failure haunt
them. It is just then I would hear these words
of Paul and test their meaning, "I can do all
things through Christ." I am glad that this
word was not a mere phrase of Paul's preaching in his great sermon on Mars' Hill. I prize
it coming out through prison chains. It lives
beyond Mamertine. It blinks not before the
block. It is ultimate triumph he speaks of, and
prisons, and chains, and axes, and graves are
unable to moderate that. The secret is all in
Christ and not in Paul. If you would seek explanation for the influence of this little hunch-
backed Hebrew on world history, don't contemplate Paul, don't sum up his privilege of school-
ing before Gamaliel, don't reckon his knowledge
of Greek and Hebrew and philosophy. You mistake when you seek Paul's power in Paul. You
see Paul. You hear Paul. The argument is
otherwhere. It is Christ, and that keeps the fact
forever dated up to every generation, for "He
is the same yesterday, to-day and forever." This
is a text for Christianity. To-day and forever,
God is our rock. We are in His shelter. From
the infinite care and solicitous love of His great
heart is reflected every experience and feeling

of joy or grief that any human soul can utter or
know. This is the great Christian confidence.
It freshens my oft-drooping hope, and restrings
my sometimes flagging ambition. Who dares
then be against me! I pluck up courage. God is
for me, what care I? After all, that is about as
startling a statement to make to one who knows
what manhood is, and how fiercely assailed it is
by evil, as any statement yet conceived. A man,
environed by a thousand corrupting influences,
with a pathway thronged by spiritual enemies,
susceptible to temptation and liable, very liable,
to go badly astray; how startling a claim this to
make, that one so weak and so exposed should
be defended and brought through conqueror, yea,
more than conqueror and possessor secure of
eternal life. Who can set explanation of this?
for this is the very heart of religion. Saul is
the natural product. Saul, blind with jealousy,
Saul, breathing out threatenings. Saul, the hating persecutor. Saul, bigot among Pharisees,
watching Stephen die for his faith in Christ,
Saul, going proudly and confidently to Damascus
to stamp out this new religion springing up
around a crucified hero. Saul is logically human. We who know men at all know Saul as a
man. We could write his history with unerr-
ing progress. But Paul is Christian resultant.
He is not logical. Our premises argue other-
where. Paul, fearless sufferer for the right.

Paul, preaching the good news to the Gentiles.
Paul, arguing for Christ in the Grecian forum
and on the mad streets of Jerusalem. Paul, ap-
pealing to Cæsar. Paul, a triumphant ship-
wrecked preacher. Paul, in Rome a prisoner for
Jesus' sake. Paul, second chief martyr of all the
Christian story, triumphant at death, breathing
there phrases of victory to word Christian triumph for suffering forever. All this I am arguing now is the eloquent history of a life that was
impelled square across human logic. There is
but one solution, and Paul wrote it for us in this
bold text, and then marched on to a life of un-
daunted achievement, and even kept it clear and
defiant in death, "I can do all things." I can
even die! Come on with your axe! "I am now
ready to be offered up, and the time of my
departure is at hand." "O death, where is thy
sting?" "O grave, where is thy victory?" "I can
do all things," I can die "through Christ which
strengtheneth me." And that word has been
written for us all here, not only by his own example, but by words of life, "My grace is sufficient for thee"; "My strength is made perfect
in weakness." O men, women, let us lay hold
of such a fact in confidence, Christ is our
strength.

> "A mighty fortress is our God,
> A bulwark never failing:
> Our helper he, amid the flood
> Of mortal ills prevailing.

For still our ancient foe
Doth seek to work us woe;
His craft and power are great,
And, armed with cruel hate,
    On earth is not his equal.

"Did we in our own strength confide,
    Our striving would be losing;
Were not the Right Man on our side,
    The Man of God's own choosing.
Dost ask who that may be?
Christ Jesus, it is He.
Lord Sabaoth is his name.
From age to age the same,
    And he must win the battle."

Luther sang that song in every dark trying time he met. It is wreathed in huge letters now round the tower of the church in Wittenberg where he lies buried. Melanchthon, his great friend and neighbor, would sing it with him. I have sat at the old rough hewn stone table in the backyard of Melanchthon's home, where they sat often together and sang the great hymn of trust when days were difficult. The eternal defiance of Christian faith. It is ours this very hour. We will not fail its use. We will fling it squarely into every conflict before us. The world may not understand how we are going to win, but Christianity never did win on the world's calculation. Christian results have been forever illogical to human syllogism. We have Christ, that is heaven's logic. We have Christ, that is God's argument. We have Christ, that is eternity's verdict.

We only await this great fact being made personal. Your case is particular. Your weakness is supplemented. Your strength is allied. There may come times when you are seemingly left alone. He knows you are strong enough to stand. I believe that profoundly. Only rarely does God ever find a soul so strong and so safely grounded that He can leave him alone. There was Job. What a character! What tragic trial of strength! What titanic struggle at balance! How pitiful in the ashes of his losses, yet how inspiring. But speaking as I am, so far on down the ages now as to get the flavor of his great victory in its reflex upon the race, and to miss much of the cutting cost of it all, I declare to you it paid mankind when God left Job alone. There was John Baptist. Trumpet of the wilderness. Maker of the road for the King's coming. But Jesus came, and all eyes left John, and turned upon the new Prophet. John languished in prison. He became even the sport of games among the indulgent rulers. His suffering was a prize. His head became a trophy. Hear him with a word, not long before a blundering headsman laid the grinning axe upon his noble shoulders, "Send a messenger and ask for me, if it is really He of whom I was preaching in the wilderness, or do we look for another." Was ever

more heart-breaking inquiry made by a prophet?
Left in prison alone. But, my friends, ever above
these He keeps watch, and forever must preserve
that greater fact that we do not trust God merely
to escape prisons, or to avoid what a narrow
world-economy calls adversity. Above you
Christ stands now. Don't you ever dare to try
to read for evidence into that, some little trifling
matter of your prosperity in houses and lands.
O, if a man can only get some reasonable assurance, that in this welter of a world, he is not
left to fight his own battle, or to muddle his way
through merely the best way he can, unhelped and
unguided. What message have we! Or have we
any at all for this big, hard-working, steel-
framed, smoke-covered, war-wracked, strike-rid-
den, Twentieth Century of ours? I am grown
weary of investigation. So much preaching of
the day seems to be an endeavor to find explanation for something that is not right. Have we
a message for life? I am sure we have. God is
with men. Christ waits to strengthen every soul
for eternal success. That is our message.

This is a matter of clear and repeated promise.
God is so very earnest about this that He has
had it run all through this great Book He has
prepared for us. He has bound Himself to us. It
is just what I would expect from a God of love
and mercy toward struggling man. He will not
suffer the enemy to prevail. I am profoundly

thankful for my confidence in God's interest. I feel no egotism in claiming the right to take this great clause from Paul's declaration and make it now my own. It was not meant for personal distinguishment. It is a Christian fact, not a Pauline distinction. God is interested in me. Not merely interested in the great general, suffering, longing, aspiring, hoping, dying race of men we call humanity. I am glad God loves the race. Upon my confidence in that I build my missionary program. But the thing that helps me most must have a personal note. The claim is not in me. I am such a tiny creature when you talk of the billion-facted fact of humanity. What a mass of mankind. How they come forever on, and lose themselves so quickly behind the hills of a close to-morrow. If humanity was marched past the great review stand, I am sure I would stumble by in my own obscurity and no notice would be taken of me. I never see the review of even a small army, but I feel the pathos of the fact that it can become monotonous, and so very many go unnoticed by to get to one who raises even a faint huzzah. O humanity! The crowding millions already gone, and those whose faces are just now looming on the horizon of to-morrow pushing me double-quick now in my middle life. Don't tell me God is interested in man. Tell me God is interested in me. I am the object of His care. That stiffens my step. That girds my

4/3 (6

courage. That was what I wanted when I was
depressed at the heavy tramplings of the myriad
feet. I was afraid my footstep would not be
heard, and I would get by unnoticed. But God
watches! And God is the God of the individual.
There is no better tonic than that. My boy
brought home a leather belt, clasped with a large
brass buckle, which he plucked from an unusually war-raked section of an awful battle-field
over which he went wading with our triumphant
troops in France. On the brass buckle stamped
in what we feel was well nigh sacrilege is, "Gott
mit uns." Why did they want it there? Because
Germany, long drilled for war, full believed with
all her drilling and preparation, men would
never go so far otherwise as they would if clothed
in divine trust. Had the brass words been true,
those brass buckles of defeated hordes would not
be trinkets now to their conquerors. If God is
with us, we cannot fail. Take that and stand.
Rest on it absolutely and be strong. You are not
too little for God's notice. I measure Christianity by God's reach, and God can reach me.
I would preach that fact into every discouraged
soul. You have a right to rest on that fact. God
is the dominant part of the declaration. This is
no proud boast of egotism Paul makes. I once
heard a great preacher say that he was not much
of an artist, but that he could draw a perfect
likeness of Paul. He stepped to a blackboard

and made a big capital "I." I dared immediately
to take issue with him. Paul's egotism died on
the road before Damascus. He found his personal way through the darkness of blindness till
he got behind the Cross of Christ. From that
moment the confident note in his preaching was
his assurance of Christ. "I can do all things,"
was sufficient word for him up till Damascus, "I
can do all things, through Christ," was his new
confidence. God and even you can do all things.
Not because of you so much. Not because of you
very much. But because of God.

No greater chapter has been written into the
human story than the one wherein the truth we
have been talking of now has been run. Nothing
else can account for the church's history as it
has made its much hindered way through every
opposition. After all, trust in God is about the
whole summary of our story. I only preach because I believe absolutely in the divine supple-
ment of human life. This great old Book of
God is about all built up around the effort to
make the availability of God an actual practical
fact in life. It was written because wandering
humanity needed a plain way out of the depths
of its failures into the presence of the Father's
house again. We are at the very heart of the
gospel now. If we can hold fast the possibilities
of our text in life just as we find it, not as we had
wished we might find it, we will have found the

secret of faith. I like to take hold of one of these
defiant songs of faith, and then march square
into the jaws of conditions I cannot explain, and
just hold on to my faith. I like to ride at sea in a
storm I cannot see beyond, if I have confidence in
my ship. I made my way one day across a large
bay in the north, in a smoke so dense I could
not see thirty feet beyond my boat. The sun, unable to shine through the gloom, cast a reddened
glow upon the quiet water. As I started on my
way aware of the ease of losing my way com-
pletely, I caught a faint shadow from the sun as
it fell across an object on the back of the boat,
and cut with a pale edge a little knot on the back
seat. I said, "I will sail into the curtain of smoke
and maintain that tiny tracery on that little spot
there as my guide." So I sailed away. I looked
no other where but to that little mark. There
was nothing to see above me or before me or behind me but that little sign. The only way I knew
I was not utterly lost in the smoke and sailing in
huge meaningless circles was by the tracery of
that shadow. I confess it was a strange and a
refreshing thing when out of the gloom at last
suddenly loomed the shore of my destination. I
propose, because of my unfailing confidence in
God, to hurl this assurance square into the face
of every trial that may arise; I can do all things,
therefore I will do all things through Christ,
which strengtheneth me. Let us make good our

faith in a difficult day. True faith is independ-
ent of facts. Don't you brand that fanaticism
till you have read religion's story to the end.
Faith has suffered much because misunderstood.
Religion is a conviction of the character of God,
and a calm resting on that alone for salvation.
We need nothing more to begin with, and everything else in our experience and fortune helps
us only in so far as it works that primary conviction more thoroughly into our characters.

How is the faith with you to-day? You, who
perhaps now are being sorely tried, I implore
you to stand firm in whatsoever lot you may be
cast. Stand square up to God's purpose in you.
His grace is sufficient for you. I believe it without qualification. I pray for strength to stand.
Anything—temptation, trial, sifting, only, O
God, rescue me from my weakness, and help me
ever to stand true on evidence of the fact that Thy
grace is sufficient, and for every man. When the
famous founder of our great Methodism came to
die his triumphant death, after the burning life
of service he had lived, he found his last words
to leave for the completion of the work he had
so earnestly set himself to do, to be this testimony. He died in the quaint little chapel house
on City Road in London. The room where he
died is a magnet to me whenever I am in London. Gathering what little strength he could
command, he twice cried out, "The best of all is,

God is with us." He fell back exhausted. A
friend bent over and moistened his lips with a
wet cloth, for they were parched with the breath
of death's near approach. "Never mind my poor
carcass," said the triumphant soul. Then paus-
ing a little he cried, "Thy clouds drop fatness."
And then, "The Lord of Hosts is with us, the
God of Jacob is our refuge." Through the night
and into the morning, where at last his dead
body lay quiet on the pillow, he whispered, and
at the end strong enough only to shape his eloquent lips, as he said on, said on, and on, right
up to death's actual arrival, "The best of all is,
God is with us. The best of all is, God is with us.
The best of all is . . ." Thanks be unto God
who giveth us the victory. Amen.

GIFT OR BARGAIN

GIFT OR BARGAIN

"Why was not this ointment sold for three hundred pence, and given to the poor?"—*John 12. 5.*

THAT is a practical question. In as practical a day as this day of ours boasts of being, such a question cannot be set aside. It must be answered. This sounds like the call for a committee of investigation, and such a committee is popular now. Few subjects are receiving keener attention to-day than waste, and while we are not noted for economy we nevertheless have been making some of our largest dividends on things a less knowing age before us threw away. Extravagant to a fault though we be, we are nevertheless efficient to the recovery of great profit in what the ignorance of a more economical yesterday never knew was waste. Why was this ointment not sold? We want an answer. If there is any reason for what looks like an unnecessary expenditure of something that in some other line would have brought greater interpretation of value, let us know. Such talk is in conclusive inflection. Practical criticism is especially commended when it carries with it a plan of corrective measure, and Judas Iscariot, the proposer of this question, seals his claim for attention by of-

fering as a suggestion a proposition which always
makes appeal to our sense of benevolence, and
draws the comparison of need against waste, by
declaring that all this might have been adminis-
tered for the relief of the poor. The whole question seems carefully drawn in terms almost axio-
matic in our ordinary interpretation of expenditure. We cannot afford to be wasteful even in
our personal expressions, if actual need stands
haunting our actions.

We must listen carefully now to this question,
or we will blunder on fundamentals. It is asked
by a man who stood before one of the finest incidents of personal affection that has ever been
recorded, and saw nothing in it but the measure
of the material idea of the service. "Why was
not this ointment sold?" It is the blundering
objection of a confident practical idea. The practical man who can risk being what he calls practical at all cost. It is an endeavor to place the
responsibility of the suffering of the poor upon
the great heart of genuine affection. Must I
believe I need to sacrifice my expression of love
and devotion to my friends, and to my highest
ideals, in order to save money enough to care for
my real benevolences? Can I ever dare a program of keeping alive my ministry to the poor,
at the price of skimping my expression of devotion? We have struck now at the very heart of
benevolence. When you lay out a program for

work among the poor, and endeavor to build it
upon the refusals of your expressions of love and
affection for those to whom your ministry is not
one of need, you will have cut the very stem on
which all benevolence grows.

Note the setting of this question. It was just
before the death of our Lord. He was on His
way to Jerusalem for the last time, and tarried
in the little village of Bethany, one of His favorite stopping places, not because it was an
attractive town, but because His friends lived
there. He had a popularity in Bethany springing from the famous incident with Lazarus. They
had arranged a modest dinner for Him at the
home of Simon the leper. When the guests were
ready for the meal Mary came quietly in and
broke a costly alabaster box, which was filled
with spikenard, and anointed the feet of Jesus
and wiped them with her hair. It was a surprise
incident. Judas arose, and sniffing the rich odor
of the nard, broke boldly into the situation which
he had no ability to appreciate and said, "Why
was not this sold?" The hypocrite! He was even
then turning over in his own mind plans by which
he could sell his Lord for a mere pittance. God
pity the man of such utilitarian view of life that
he cannot see beyond the cost mark; the man who
lives his life in the bounds of market quotations.
He knows the value of spikenard. He always
carries the last market quotation. No smell of

ointment ever escapes his calculation. Life is
written in figures to him. He tags things. He
knows arithmetic, but he never has a poetic idea.
He can compute interest, but he will not admit
value in sentiment. This is serious preachment
for this day of ours, when so many men are actually sacrificed to business, and stunted in their
moral development because by nature they are
shut off from all the deeper things of life. You
may think at first reading that this suggestion
of Judas was a sound word of economy, but you
will discover before you have tried to live with it
very long that it is a perfectly sterile plan to
build life around. You cannot afford to starve
your higher self if you are to expect to find that
self really ministrant among men. There are
some things you must do for your own life if you
are to keep it where it will ever care to minister
to others.

There are two simple yet significant observa-
tions I wish to deduce from this incident, which
I shall endeavor to make interpretive of it as constructive of best life. My first thought is, that it
might have been sold. That liability run up
against this lovely little, yet cherished, story,
makes me wonder just how much poorer the
world would be now had mere economy pre-
vailed in this case. How much would real benevolence have lost had they saved this spikenard
for benevolence then? I can believe that had

Judas but known of Mary's possession before she broke her precious box, he might have presented for her a very difficult case. She was tender-hearted. She had doubtless already been giving to the poor of her village, and I am sure she knew a great deal more about them than did Judas. But had he known she had saved up some precious ointment, he might have called her attention to some specific cases, all of which she well knew, and with them have made a most searching appeal to her heart. It is too bad to pour our three hundred pence in wasted fragrance, when there are some who are really hungry. Why don't you sell this ointment and bestow the money on the poor? Yes, it might have been sold. Suppose it had been. Many a fine rich intention has been sold and distributed. Many a genuine high purpose has been turned aside and merely cashed in. What would the world have gained had it been so here? This would at least have been a dull and unnoticed feast, and would have found no place in the Bible, and this little box, whose fragrance was loosed to the whole world, before hard-edged careful calculating practicality could cash it and invest it, would have been interpreted as three hundred pence and fed into a few hungry mouths, and been heard of no more. As it was, it found an ever-widening fragrance to sweeten the genuine devotion of the world, and inspire forever a benevolence and a ministry not to be measured by mere market values, but by an ever ascending series of good influences.

O what extravagance it had been had the economy of Judas that day sold that spikenard. Three hundred pence. Poor little price, and the thing about it too is that it was all it was worth. Whenever you actually cash things in you put them in bounds where ordinary bookkeepers can keep their accounts. Three hundred pence will buy just a certain number of meals of victuals. The actual computed values of things look small when you are really looking for life quotation. There is real judgment on a man who stands near an incident like this. Judas could see nothing but waste. That is the blunder of worldliness. It cheapens devotion. It cannot understand love. I am glad it can't. Love never was intended to be understood. There are plenty of things to understand. There are plenty of things which admit of calculation. It is good and altogether helpful to have some things among us that will not admit of analysis. I am glad to see a man who knows only market values confounded at values sometimes. Judas cheapens himself when he suggests his idea before this incalculable expression. He looks like a child reaching for the moon. His arms are too short. Three hundred pence for such a story. Imagine it. All the suggestion has done has been to cheapen the suggester of it in the estimation of the world. He knew the value of spikenard. That's all some folks know. And there is so much more. Alabaster and spikenard were the very cheapest things in this transaction, and yet Judas saw nothing else.

It might have been sold! Suppose it had been. I wish I could get that liability so said here now that its significance might catch attention in the real issues of all our lives. Did you ever try to picture this world with such scenes as this all contracted out, and sold, even for benevolence? Figure coldly right into the human story with all such incidents as this commercialized. Three hundred pence for this story! Take your checkbook and try to actually buy out the really great heart-facts of life. Try to reduce the love, and the romance, and the heroism of life to finance. Make bold to approach with your bid those fine stories of the faith of men and women who have died in their honor, to leave to us all a gift that will outlast eternity. Buy out now these great world stories. That fine young Huguenot lover in the days of the crazed hunting of faith. You remember the scene on which the artist has fixed his genius, when, hunted from the mountain fastness where he had been hiding, he is taking leave of his loved one, and she, in fear of his personal loss, is begging him to be willing to wear the little badge on his arm which safety required, but which really meant his renuncia-

tion of faith. He straightened himself to say
that great word which has been again the poured
out ointment for the world's life that could not
be bought, "I could not love thee, dear, so much,
loved I not honor more." That is the fragrance
that was not for sale. It might have been sold,
but the world is richer to-day because it was
not.

It has been written in master story in Silas
Marner. That book caries no finer word, in all
the great things carried there, than that great
crisis which came to that tried man when the
little girl whose life had become the object of his
long abused devotion, was left to decide between
her own father, who had meanly deserted her
and left her to die; and then came back finding
her grown to fine girlhood in the care of this poor
old friend whose friendship was built up out of
a desperation that came from the wreckage of
false friends. The father came offering her fortune and a palace home to come back to, and
Marner, with nothing to offer her but his honest
love; no money, just a living; no position, just
honor; no palace, just a clean cottage; with
nothing but these to offer, that old-time miser
stood trembling to see what the girl would do.
He was saved to a genuine faith in humanity, as
the girl ran, and leaping into his glad old arms
chose him because he loved her. It might have
been sold! But thank God how often love has

absolutely turned itself away from barter, and chosen to stand stark in its own genuine worth.

I have thought how the world's story would look just now, aflame with the dawn, costly though it be, of the greatest day human rights have ever seen, had this bargaining possibility been consummated in the crisis of those tragic days, through which we have just made our hard but victorious way. It might have been sold! We can say that terrible possibility to-day, even through the blood of millions of men. We can say it against the triumph of our cause, and with the liberties of mankind in better position than ever before in all the story of the world's struggles. Will we dare try to think now that it might all have been sold. Suppose Belgium had sold out! That great pressing confident host that never carried a suspicion that there was anywhere a barrier that could even hinder it, not to say stop it! Trained to expect victory, they came tramping straight up to the boundary of little Belgium, and started to push back the gates. Offers of immense import to the nation were made. The offerers never imagined they could be denied. There is no finer story of national honor written than that which was graven forever into the world's heroism when little Belgium, great Belgium, immortal Belgium, refused to sell her honor. She chose to be trampled down in suffering and desolation, and if need be death, but in self-respect and imperishable honor, rather than to live enriched in territory perhaps, but shorn of her good name. To-day, with her king and the shattered remnant of her noble army returned to their sad, but glorious, residence amid the broken remnants of their once beautiful land, the whole world is joining to thank God for their faithfulness. It might have been sold.

The really great stories of the world's finest experiences have been written hard up against the tragic liability of the alternative Judas draws in this lovely little story from Bethany. It is in such alternative we can best write triumph. This after all is the victory of human character. The stories of all great victories have threaded their ways through grave liabilities. Where is the soul who has come on into life very far to whom this is unfamiliar talk? Temptation has forever spread before us the alternative on which we make or break. Your honor was at stake! Your virtue was in the balance! Your whole influence was liable! They might have been sold! Three hundred pence. A bit of dazzling pleasure. An hour of delirious delight. A gain of a few golden dollars. The applause of some false friends. These are the offers when bargains have been struck that have sold out of life the rich things. Three hundred pence have many times been accepted. There is supreme inspiration in our never-failing Lord and Mas-

ter when He stood on the mountain and was offered all the world as a price. Knowing what
we do to-day, in terms translated into human
courage by that scene of triumph of His, we never
stop to reckon the size of the price offered. Little matters the price when tragedy supreme is at
stake. Three hundred pence would have been as
much to offer Him then as a world, for the
tragedy of it all lay not in the price that was
made, but in the fact that He might have sold
out.

All this brings me where I can now say
quickly, for it has been partially said already,
the second thing I wish to emphasize. It might
have been sold, but it wasn't. I thank God for
that. I take courage for my own life in whatever
it may have to meet, when I see how a calamity
was avoided into a blessing. The only man who
went away from that feast in the home of Jesus'
friends in Bethany with criticism, was the man in
whose heart burned a faithlessness and a treachery that would at a soon coming day offer even his
Lord for sale, and stand counting out his paltry
thirty pieces of silver at first, as though he had
struck another bargain. If it was an extravagance to pour out that oil there as Judas claimed
it was, love will admit the guilt of extravagance.
Love and affection never did pose as economists.
There are times when economy sounds like
treason. There are times when it sounds like

pure stinginess. When men write the definition
of extravagance around the bare lines of mere
duty, love will always be extravagant. The
spikenard might have been sold, but it wasn't.
Hence, instead of becoming a mere ration for a
few hungry folks in Bethamy, and being de-
voured and forgotten along with a great many
other three hundred pence that have been eaten
into oblivion; instead of merely rationing that
treasure it has become inspiration for the benevolences of a whole world. I am indeed grateful for
the fine ministries that have escaped the sales-
man. I thank God for those fine impulses of life
that get themselves expressed before the sheer
economist can estimate them and stop them. The
world is full of fragrance to-day because noble,
self-sacrificing men and women have always
poured rich life out upon it. "Why was not this
sold?" has forever been asked of folks who have
in genuine sacrifice sought to make the world
better. It is a question you can see no answer
for, unless you take your stand squarely on the
ground that it has no justice in its asking. We
need to heroically walk out to such living that
wherever we go among men there shall attend us
the fragrance of a ministry that overleaps all
coldly calculated service and makes registry in
true and uncalculating devotion. The best things
of life are those that, overflowing all calculations
of value, have purchased a larger life than man

has ever dared stake out in his fondest dreams. Thank God for sacrifices that have been made which never could have been bargained for. Thank God for Jesus Christ, to Whom this bargaining hypocrite who dared inject the proposition of his crass commercialism into the incident of this loving company of friends in Bethany, dared set a price of thirty pieces of silver, but Whose worth can never be known till all the countless hosts of the redeemed shall have sung their eternal songs of redemption about the throne. Thank God! Thank God for love that overleaps all calculations and asks no rules of conduct but love. "Why was not this sold for three hundred pence and given to the poor?" Because it was not for sale.

YET

THIS STRIKING FIGURE IN BRONZE WAS MADE
BY ALFRED NYGARD AS A NEW INTERPRETA-
TION OF HOPE. IT WAS SUGGESTED BY THE
SERMON "YET" AS PRINTED HERE.

YET

"I shall yet praise him."—*Psa. 42. 11.*

THIS is the text in ordinary for thanksgiving. It has furnished the ever recurring basis for sermons on thanksgiving all down the years. I would in no way seem to criticize such interpretation when I dare to wrench it square away from all that, and set it facing a much more vigorous expression of life than mere thankfulness. There are a multitude of verses in the Bible where praise is taught. The spirit of it is everywhere. If you shall turn to your concordance to find this verse you could only find it by the prominent word used, which is "praise." Who would ever look for "yet"? There are so many yets in the Bible you could trace no verse by it. But to me the strong word in this text is "yet." My chief affection for this verse is based upon that persistent qualifying word which stands just ahead of praise, there. Yet! Look at it. Listen to it. What a grip it has. How impossible to beat it off. How it fans a spark to a flame. How it laughs at persecution. How it goes on through difficulty. How it holds fast in trial. How it glows in darkness. How tireless it is yet! Yet! Yet! I shall yet praise Him. Take heart, my

125

friend, the present must not overwhelm you. To-day must not claim your surrender. Don't measure your life by the little eddy we call, now. Yet! See how far you can look down the ages. You have a long way to go. Thank God the Psalmist put this word in here and made so much more out of this phrase than it would have been, had he written it, "I will praise him," which I contend now is about all the interpretation it has ever received. There is strength in "yet," when you set it doggedly against some of the places in life where praise does not seem to come by nature. It is the spirit we need in our souls when opposition which seems so easily fatal to so many, rises against us. It is the stimulant for hours that hang heavy when God seems far away. "Yet" looks ahead, and with no reckoning of what the distance is that shall yet require negotiation, goes on confidently. Maybe I don't know much about the souls of folks, but what little I do know is enough to make certain to me that what this familiar text can contribute to the world will be done at the point of this little determined word. Praise we are willing to give, but to persist in believing always that justification for praise will certainly arrive even in our lot, is eternal tonic. This is abounding hope founded on faith. Unquestioning trust of God. Unfaltering waiting for him. It was that tremendous leap of assurance which John Baptist

called out through the trouble of prison and
seeming neglect even to his Master and said:
"Art thou he that shall come, or do we look for
another?" That wasn't despondency. That was
a word that was so full of faith that it declared
that even if Christ failed him, he went on looking. I know, my friends, how hard life often
seems to you to be, but I preach a faith that fixes
hope so confidently in our souls that it will forever declare, "Maybe I can't praise him just now,
and here, but I will yet do so."

> "Here I'll raise mine Ebenezer,
>   (It has surely been hard thus far,)
> But I hope by thy good pleasure,
>   Safely to arrive at home."

Hope never looks so much like hope as it does
when it comes forth strong in a hopeless sort of
a place. Over in the prophecy of Hosea it speaks
of "a door of hope even in the valley of Achor."
The refreshing fact in the much unnoticed passage is, that no one ever expected hope there.
I confess that hope isn't hope in the expected
places. It takes Achor to furnish a proper setting. All the way along the human story God
has been doing His divine best to write that fact
to men. O I wish I could preach unfailing hope
into the hearts of the folks I know. I shall yet
praise Him! When the city of Messina was
tumbled down by the rough hands of that earth-
quake, and multitudes of dead lay in the ruins

down every toppled street, there came out of it
all a story that thrilled the whole world. I was
walking amid the ruins of the city a few days
later and saw the house, and have a picture of
the heroic lad. In the tumbling of their home
which was but one in a solid row of brick build-
ings, the timbers so fell as to make a tiny tent
over the three children, thus holding the pouring
brick and stone from crushing them at once.
Everything had fallen. The dense darkness
settled over them, as they crouched under tons
and tons of brick and stone of the ruins. Certain
death seemed their lot. But the lad saw at last,
as his eyes became used to the darkness, a tiny
point of light. He resolved to follow that spark.
With all the genius and patience hope can devise
he set to work to carefully pick away the brick
and mortar with his bare fingers. Always that
one tiny spark of light must be preserved. It is
a story to challenge admiration. They had a
few onions and some olive oil which had tumbled
with them into their strange protection. For
fourteen indescribable days that boy, thirteen
years of age, held faithfully to that ray of light,
until at last, with his fingers worn to the bone,
and bleeding his young life out on every brick
he moved, he broke through into the day and
deliverance. His name, with the two young sisters whose deliverance his faithfulness had won,
were sent to the whole world, as headline news.

But it was after all a very old story among men,
not often worked out in just such a setting, but
worked out in experience.   The salvation of
hope—

"In the suburb, in the town,
    On the railway, in the square,
Came a beam of goodness down,
    Doubling daylight everywhere;
Peace now each for malice takes,
    Beauty for his sinful weeds,
For the angel Hope aye makes
    Him an angel whom she leads."

I like to hear about hope.   I like to preach
about hope to a world such as this.   It is so vital,
and so virile.   Yes, I mean virile, and that is the
sufficient reason for my choosing this text for a
sermon on hope.   "Yet," has such a determined
sound, and seems to put such a flavor of con-
quest in hope that I like it, for hope has always
been represented so delicate and non-resistant.
The artists put such delicate robes upon her
shoulders and paint her so resigned in attitude,
as she sits on the darkening circle of a world,
holding a harp with the strings all broken.   But
no artist would ever make such a picture if you
would furnish him this text for a description,
"Come, artist, I want you to paint me a picture
of Hope."   "I shall be glad to do so," says he,
"but what does it look like?"   And I wrote out
for him these words, "I shall yet praise him."
There flashed at once to his conception a picture

of heroics. No immaculate garments for Hope.
No delicate face, but rather a stern scarred face.
Garments, coarse and torn. Sandals, heavy and
crude. An eye that burned like a star. And all
this not to sit in mere waiting through desolation, but rather to come fighting triumphantly
through difficulty. Whatever may be done by
tears or sorrow or temptation or weariness or
study or endurance, there is yet something better
than all these. How hard we work to find this
better way. It puzzles us often, for life does
carry such crushing loads. Came a woman to
me one day trudging through troubles so deep
and bitter we knew no words to tell her hardship. She was trying to fight out some clear
explanation for it all. The best we could
together do was to agree that somehow some
finer end might be attained. It is the very best
we can do with many of our tangled experiences.
We are at sea constantly trying to reconcile our
conceptions of a God of love and human trouble.
But through it all there seems reposing in the
human heart a confidence in the power and purpose of God, carrying the universe onward to its
final perfection and glorification. If we could
but once leap to a vantage peak, as Beecher put
it onewhere, and brushing the tears from our
eyes see down the clamoring ages. If we could
catch to our ears the thunder and clash of all the
battles. If we could see the whole world storm-

wracked and tossed on the shoulders of a wind
that blew from heaven to heaven, it would be an
unspeakable gladness to see at the end the glowing colors of complete triumph for the good.
Convince me that storm-tossed and broken and
battered, I am nevertheless making progress.
Let me know, that heart-broken and burdened to
breaking, there is surely a balm for every wound.
Assure me that with all, the storm by its very
fierceness is driving me nearer home. Then I
will hold the rudder firm, I will watch every
cloud in defiance, I will sing at every raging sea,
"I shall yet praise him!" Yet! Do your worst.

How truly vital all this is as a testimony to
the great distinguishment of the human soul. It
hurls me into things with a meaning. It shows
human life as human. It is the breath of to-morrow which breathes life into my weary to-day.
If I am to be told that I am only that which I
have been, life will lose its chief inspiration to
me. If on my poor grave they shall carve a stone
to tell what I was, it will mean no more to me
than those heavy words they laid the broken body
away with, "ashes to ashes, dust to dust." Not
much comfort in that. It sounds like that poverty we all recognize and try to express kindly
by saying, "It was the best he could do." Don't
leave "yet" off my grave-stone. Fling me on, on!
Not what I was! Not what I have been! God
forgive me! What I have been, humbles me in

repentant appeal for pardon. But what I shall be, makes me leap to my feet even across my grave. Men can breathe that. It is the eternal tonic of religion. Listen to it, you tired soul. I am not very old, and I have not had very much experience perhaps in this crowding world of ours, but I have had enough experience to thoroughly convince me that it is the lead of the past which crushes the life out of men. The past mangles our spirits. It steals our joys. It hushes our songs. But I tell you that the buoyancy of life abounds in the fact that the grave is not shut. Yet! Yet! is a wholesome word to give to a world like this. I can wait beyond the storm of time. The blue has already flickered through, and thrills my courage. "I shall yet praise Him." Give me faith in that and I can live and wait. Yet! I submit, it has saved the world. God has long governed us with it. It is what I am looking for that keeps me going. It lifts me to the mountain. It strengthens me for the valley. It soothes me to slumber at night. It spurs me to my duty again when morning comes. To live at all I must catch the breath of to-morrow. Yesterday is musty to my soul. I am alive. The very things we want most seem to be yet hitherbound. "Yesterday is for gratitude and regret. To-day is for contentment and work. To-morrow is for hope and trust." "When I awake in Thy likeness," we read from the Bible

with relish. Did the audacity of such a hope
ever strike your mind? Had we been mere logi-
cians we had long ago drawn our conclusions,
and been choked by death. But we have been
forever setting our purpose against even our experiences, and with the determination of the
Psalmist's "yet," have marched against whatever
life brought us. God has human ultimate in
hand. We are not in to-day, but to-morrow.
What we shall be is reserved for heaven's vision.
In such an economy as that which prevails here
the problem of human life is, how to unfold mankind and bring him to his perfect nature.

> "Here where perhaps alone
>   I conquer or I fail!
> Here, o'er the dark deep blown,
>   I ask no perfumed gale;
> I ask the unpampering breath,
>   That fits me to endure,
> Chance, and victorious Death,
>   Life, and my doom obscure,
> Who know not whence I am sped,
> Nor to what port I sail.

> "And though within me here,
>   Hope lingers unsubdued,
> 'Tis because airiest cheer
>   Suffices for her food;
> As some adventurous flower,
>   On savage crag-side grown,
> Seems nourished hour by hour,
>   From its wild self alone,
> So lives inveterate Hope,
> On her own hardihood."

Humanity is balanced by hope. Job, sitting in the bitter ashes of the loss of everything he held dear, yet strangely sustained. Paul, with a soul that could respond to a world's call, yet chained to a poor diseased body, a mortal handicap, but heroically keeping the faith and making triumph eternal. A vast multitude of men and women with ideals broken, ambitions crushed, and purposes thwarted. Looking at life with all it has to confound us, I still see hope emerging from despair, and pulling its feet out of the slough of despond, fighting its hindered but always onward way to ultimate victory. I would that it were in my power to find convincing words to say to every one who may have lost heart in these difficult days, to hope on. He is sure of being least deluded who has courage to do so. For "the most ingenious hope is nearer truth than the most rational despair." I know disappointment is real, and life seems to carry an empty basket for a multitude, but while God lives hope cannot die. Late one wearied afternoon, during the most distressing period of the war, Albert of Belgium stood at a window in the City Hall in Furnes watching the setting sun. There was upon his face all the evidence of the heavy anxiety which he had so long borne, and the sunset but enforced the thought in his heart and drove the lines more keenly into his features. The coming night with its settling gloom seemed to be the evident unwritten history of the land he loved, and his depression was very great. Just as the sun disappeared and darkness seemed to triumph, the King with courageous hope which was reading into the dark his country's story, spoke thus, "But the night is not eternal, and when it is gone there comes another day, bringing with it a new glad morning."

"I shall yet praise him." I might as well begin now.

WARMING HIMSELF

WARMING HIMSELF

"And Peter stood with them, and warmed himself."—John 18. 18.

KEEPING warm is a perfectly proper thing to do, as a mere physical exercise. We are all in full sympathy with the folks who have a hard time with the primary problem of warmth. I witnessed an interesting incident recently at a dinner I was attending, whereat a representative company of business men sat about the tables, for the consideration of some matters of importance pertaining to the general business situation. The matter of stealing coal from cars was talked about in general conversation because it had been an advertised condition of a serious nature. There came passing around the tables a long petition to the authorities to enforce the law, and posted at the head of the sheet was a perfectly clear photograph of a group of children busy at some loaded cars carrying away the coal. The situation was really bad. It was unusually significant then because we were in the midst of one of winter's coldest periods, and doubtless there was a great amount of downright thievery carried on under the guise of needed relief, which plea of course made good newspaper matter. There were very few names on the long paper. I

sat next to the president of the meeting and it
was his conduct that fastened my interest to the
whole incident. He read the request, and said
without intention of being heard, and indeed ad-
dressing himself in the statement, "I don't see
any reason why the law should not be enforced."
He took his pen, and began to vibrate his hand
over the dotted line for his signature, but did
not touch the pen-point to write. He stopped,
lifted his pen and said, "No, I won't sign that,"
and having finished his conversation with himself, passed the paper along. I am only saying
that warming himself under some circumstances
may be the very thing in which we hold an in-
tense and sympathetic interest. It all depends
upon who it is who happens to be cold. How he
got cold. And whether or not there are attendant circumstances which would argue that it
might be even more fitting for him to remain
cold, than to turn aside and engage in what may
be very, very small business, merely warming
himself. It might be a sure testimony that he
was not doing his full share of the work available, and thus became chilled. Working folks
don't suffer from the cold. These fires you see
burning near working men on real jobs are not
for the workers, but for the fellows who stand
around. I noticed the other day the white
streaming steam rising from some racing water
which ran along the spill-way from a mill beside

a solidly ice-bound river. The water in the race
was at work. I saw in the big lounging room of
Henry Ford's home a characteristic motto. It
is cut in big rough letters in a great unhewn
log which spans the long space over a wonderful fireplace, "He warms himself twice who cuts
his own wood." So it may be true, that the attendant fact upon the cold temperature which
has come over the man who needs warming, may
be found to be that he had not been doing any
very real work, and plain work might be not
only a good plan for fuel conservation, but also
a worth-while fact for the conserver. A task
that is not strenuous enough to keep the jobber
warm should never be accepted in winter months.
It is certain in this text that Peter had turned
in among some loafers who were sitting about the
neighborhood of the court. You will note the
incident as following the record that "Peter fol-
lowed afar off." That sounds cold. He certainly had blue hands before he came anywhere
near the court-room. You cannot keep warm to
any crucial situation by any such afar removed
position. You either follow afar off, because you
are cold already, or you get cold just as soon as
you begin to lag behind. Close up interest to real
events either keeps you warm or renders you unconscious of the smaller fact of your personal
temperature.

Let me explain how this now fascinating clause

of familiar scripture was separated to my attention, and at once became a helpful guide to my
thought and purpose. An unusually readable
article on religious conditions was published in
the Atlantic Monthly, titled with the words of
my text. It was from the ready pen of Dr. Joseph
H. Odell, and was a severe criticism of the attitude of Peter as a good representation of the
church to-day. The only fault I would suggest
with his contention would be that Peter does not
represent all the church as he stands with his
shivering purpled hands held out to the coals of
a tiny fire. The Outlook declared in comment
on the article that we must not forget "that other
disciple," who never stopped, but was so close
in interest to his Lord that he pushed right on
and remained close beside Jesus during all those
tragic and significant hours. If you want a real
picture of the church out of this incident here,
you must not be confined to one type, and expect
good results. Dark shadows require high lights.
I will not accept Peter standing shivering outside there beside that flaring little fire, trying to
get some warmth through a cold body that was
sustained by a heart that was cold to the situation, as a type for the Church of Christ to-day.
He does, however, present before us a most
thought-provoking fact for consideration in liability both for the church and for the church-
man.

The article started out with an interesting quotation from Cyprian, Bishop of Carthage in the Third Century. He was writing a letter to his friend Donatus. In the letter he said, "This is a cheerful world as I see it from my fair garden, and from under the shadows of my vines. But if I could ascend some high mountain, and look out over the wide lands, you know very well what I would see. Brigands on the highways. Pirates on the seas. Armies fighting. Cities burning. In the amphitheaters, men murdered to pleased applauding crowds. Selfishness and cruelty and misery and despair, under all the roofs. It is a bad world, Donatus, an incredibly bad world. But I have discovered in the midst of it, a quiet and holy people who have learned a great secret. They have found a joy which is a thousand times better than any of the pleasures of our sinful life. They are despised and persecuted, but they care not. They are masters of their souls. They have overcome the world. These people, Donatus, are Christians, and I am one of them."

Now there is an escape described there for which we all have felt a yearning at times, which yearning was doubtless dictated by cowardice or weariness. But we know most positively that it is not, and never can be, a fair picture of a Christian. We were not called in this world to avoid its difficulties. During the war I was

amused and interested as well in an incident
which took place in one of our western States
where had settled a religious colony whose convictions were at discord with everything national.
They decided to leave America and migrate to
some place of actual peace. I don't know where
they chose to go, but some western editor who
was possessed of an aggressive idea of every conviction of righteousness wrote an editorial on
those folks and entitled it "Good-bye, Jim. Here's
Your Hat." Christianity is not engaged in moving away from the troublesome matters of life.
Christianity is not a retreat. Christianity is not
a search for a new Garden of Eden. Christianity
is a victory. Christianity is a determination to
restore again the Garden. Christianity faces
life, just as it is, and sets itself with all its re-
sources and determinations, even with sacrifice,
to bring that life up to what it ought to be. I
am greatly pleased to know that the good old
Bishop Cyprian was not justly represented, when
this one letter to his friend Donatus was quoted.
He wearied of the shadow of his vine. He was
uncomfortable in the comfort of his retreat. The
most uncomfortable place in this world for a
vital genuine character is a comfortable seat.
Cyprian came forth from that soft-shaded retreat
and actually met the heroic death of a martyr for
the faith he sought to match against the wrongs
of his day. Thus did he write over the message

of that comfortable letter Dr. Odell used as a sample, the strong and outstanding fact which we have always believed was the very heart of genuine Christianity, that after all there was under his quiet conduct even when he sought retirement, a basal conviction that would laugh even at death, and go forth to die rather than sit in personal ease against his convictions.

The genuine interest, however, to me in this text, is not in the line of the article just mentioned. The preacher is inefficient. When Dr. Odell argues that, I would not seem to dispute his contention. The ordinary problems of the dull pull of circumstances, as life had been presenting them to us for many years, with all the lack of the heroic, and tragic and unusual, which so suddenly sprang into everything in life, with the fury of the great war, had doubtless dulled us all. O the pull of the ordinary! I have come to believe it is after all really more trying than the pull of the extraordinary. It is so monotonous. The days are all so alike. It is so unromantic. Things come on just as they were planned. I know full well that in the ordinary times, we preachers did not meet the real demand.

Neither am I particularly interested in the counter attack made upon Dr. Odell's position by the naming of some preachers who were outstanding influences, and seeking to weigh them against the utterly overwhelming needs of our crucial day. Who, that has ever dared stand before and preach into the face of these difficult days, has not felt as the famous one long ago, "a voice of one crying in the wilderness"? I am sure every earnest man who has dared preach of late has gone straight home to his study from his pulpit, many, many times, sick at heart and depressed in soul because he has known all too well how utterly weak and unworthy he was. Never has preaching been so hard. But I have learned too much, in my reading of history, to dare pass judgment upon the preaching of God's Word. I know, as I begin to look back along the line of the men whose preaching did mold the world, that much in their own day, they were despised and pitied and rejected, and often actually carted out and killed for their efforts. Of course there are not many of us getting killed for preaching any more, which fact may not be laid entirely as a charge against our inability as preachers, but may likewise find a partial explanation in the fact that the general public has more sense than it once had.

The absorbingly interesting idea, however, that comes to me, as I separate this clause, and hold it against this actual day of ours is, the careless selfishness of any soul in great calling days like these, who could be so utterly disengaged as to be warming himself, merely warming himself.

These are genuinely hard days for a real man
to catch very much of a self-serving thought.
Who am I to think that I should crowd myself
in close to a nice little fire and hold out my cold
hands? I must have some real good reason before I dare push in anywhere in search of personal comfort now. What claim has my personal
comfort for attention? I was on the "California
Limited," "migrating with the rich," as a friend
of mine described it. I was only going a short
distance, but I never told them. We went out
of our winter-swept station on time. The eager
travelers were well supplied with literature
printed on warm yellow paper, adorned with
swaying palms and basking beaches. Hurry,
hurry, hurry, was the song of the clicking rails,
as they fell asleep headed for the land of summer
in winter. When morning dawned, the big red
sun awakened me as it looked over a wintered
hill into my window, and I noticed we were standing quietly out in the country. That train does
not stop. It must not stop, for these travelers are
going somewhere. I arose, dressed, ate my break-
fast, plunged into my book, and still the train
stood. I could hear the ringing hammers of the
workmen, and that tired sounding squeak of es-
caping steam under my car. We were four hours
late when we started again. A woman just across
the aisle ventured some remarks, and then read
the folders describing summer-land again, and

looked out the cold windows across the snow-covered fields. She asked me if I thought there was any possible chance of the train making up those lost four hours. I assured her they still had half a continent to cross, and there was doubtless some chance to recover some time. Soon she was back with her question again, and seemed so nervous and eager that I supposed she was hoping to make a close connection there and asked her how much time she would have to count on. "O, I will be there all winter and spring, but I want to be sure and get there on time." Warming herself! On time to lie in the warm sand under kind sunshine. Almost four hours lost in so trifling a matter as the break-down of an engine. Men were out there in the night-cold, lying on their backs under an old simmering engine with smoking torches and ringing hammers, and clinging wrenches, when she might have been warming herself. All this brings accusation against our day. "And he stood warming himself." What of it? Little heroics in that. It don't sound strong or even permissible in a day when every fire we build is in the protection of a sacrifice the like of which no generation has ever been defended by. The price that has been paid that I might inherit the peace and privilege of this hour spoils my enjoyment of it. It is actually harder to vindicate our right to inherit such a day as this is, than it was to go out and die to bring it in. All this spoils the comfort of my fire. It discomforts my comfort. It shames my selfishness. You cannot explain Peter's blame away. The outstanding thing that blows away every concealing smoke that may have enshrouded the cold coward there, was that just inside the door there was Jesus Christ in the hands of His enemies, and His friends were most all gone. When a world-crisis is on who will dare plead square into the heart of such a fact that first of all he was compelled to consider his shivering temperature? One time in the passion of an appeal which John B. Gough was making, he struck the table with his fist and broke two bones of his hand, and never knew it till the evening was gone and his hand had begun to swell. One day a Roman army was so utterly engaged in the battle they fought that an earth-quake which shook the very rocks under their feet was not noticed by them. When the great mine at Messines Ridge in France was blown at 3:10 o'clock one morning, it was heard just out-side London by Lloyd George, who was listening for it. I met a young fellow from the lines two days later in a hospital who was within three hundred yards of the edge of the mine when it went off and never heard it, so absorbed was he in the passion of the moment. What is the matter with this apostle Peter, who in a crisis when heaven and earth were bending to attention; when devils were delirious with delight that they had found at last the way to put to flight this Nazarene Who had been bothering hell so badly; when heaven, with all the eternal significance to mankind before it, was watching the rapid consummation of the salvation of the Lamb slain from before the foundation of the world! I say what is the matter with a man who under such pressure should ever recognize that he was cold. When great things are to do personal convenience should find no voice. The presence of genuine crisis should make a healthy life unconscious of personal welfare. "Peter stood warming himself." You must take care of yourself, you know! How much I have heard it. It can be done. Peter can get warm. But what if he does? He would never have been cold had he remained close up to Christ Whom now he so easily denied. Denial is cold work. To a man like Peter, more than a little fire of chips was needed if he was to be warmed. His heart was cold. The life that really makes good in a world like this is the one so utterly enamored of its task that it recognizes little of itself. A few years ago that intrepid Arctic explorer, Steffanson, set sail again in a determined effort to drive his much hindered way into the frozen mysteries of the north. He knew the liabilities. He knew the sufferings. He knew the long siege of it all. He knew how the folks at home became con-

cerned and sent out parties of rescue. So as he
vanished away, the very last word he sent back
to civilization was this heroic appeal, "Don't
rescue me prematurely." I know full well how
hard this thing is to which I go, don't worry over
me. That was indeed the choice of a full espousal
of a difficult task.

I know full well that you do not have to enter
into the great world-struggles. You can turn
aside and build you a little fire and warm yourself. You can keep perfectly snug and comfortable. You might even need to fan your flushed
cheek to keep from getting overheated at times.
No, you don't need to enter into the great world
tragedies, and burn with their fierce passion.
You can sit aside there with Peter and poke the
little embers of a selfish fire as a substitute for
the glowing fire of espousal in the great causes
at stake. You can if you will, keep yourself on
the cool side of every great question that comes
before men for decision. There are many, many
folks who do so, and you will not be lonesome
there, warming yourself. In every great world
crisis there are many who are cold to the issue.
It is human prerogative.

"Men can live and lie reclined
  On the hills, like Gods together, careless of mankind,
  They can lie beside their nectar while the bolts are hurled,
  Far below them in the valley, while the clouds are lightly
        curled
Round their golden houses, girdled with the gleaming world,

While they smile in secret, looking over wasted lands,
Blight and famine, plague and earthquake, roaring deeps
    and fiery sands,
Clanging fights and flaming towns, and sinking ships, and
    playing bands,
But they smile."

"Peter stood warming himself." I know that. We stand to-day when the crisis is drawn. The clash of conflict still roars in our ears. It will not die away among the troubled hills for many years. The chill of severe suffering sweeps the world. Strong men are dying, women are weeping, children are starving, civilization is in mad confusion. Can it be possible in such a day there will be anywhere on earth one single chilled brother who will be so wrapped up in himself as to realize that his little carcass is cold? Cold! How did it get cold? There is surely enough of interest these days to keep live folks warm. Warming himself! What if he didn't get warm? What if he remained cold? Plodding our hard and hardening way through one of the world's crucial periods, there is only one real question to ask about us, and it has nothing to do with the thermometer. It is about getting our work done. Not that you could not eat, or that you did not enjoy yourself, or that you could not keep warm. These the world will never ask concerning you. I may be comfortably toasting myself before a lovely fire. But the day is passing swiftly by, and life is running fast away, and

my fire will soon burn to ashes, and the night
will come. That night once come no one will ever
trouble to ask about my temperature. Did anyone notice just how warm Brother Rice was as
the night came on and the darkness fell? No!
No! These things don't matter.

Peter's fame in the world-story is not based
upon this trying thing we have been looking at
now when he seemed to suffer a strange break-up
of his best qualities. I am so glad that this was
merely a season of disorganization that came
over him. He does not live in the history of the
world in the selfish glow of this little smudge,
hunched up and shivering, off to one side, from
the real point of interest. He whose name has
actual place heroic in the world, is the apostle
who, recovering himself from that warming
group, went boldly out even unto bitterest persecution for the faith he possessed, and who for the
faith he dared preach into the teeth of official
persecution had to meet genuine suffering, but
flinched not, nor sought again the separated comforts of a warming fire, but went straight to his
duty, and met death for it. They say he died by
crucifixion which by his own choice was accomplished head downward as evidence of his un-
worthiness to even die in manner similar to his
Lord and Master, Whom then he was so eager to
acknowledge, as before in denial he had been so
solicitous to warm himself beside. This is the

qualification upon which this man's character
finds its place and keeps its forever increasing
power in the human story where men are being
enlisted in the causes of honor. I come now
calling to you, any of you, who in such a day as
this may have been willing to listen to the seduc-
tive arguments couched in a comfortable fire before which you might cuddle down and forget
the fight. In the name of high duty, don't you
think it is time now to let that little fire go out,
and forget yourself a bit, and plunge whole-
heartedly into the world's great struggle? There
is so much to do. There is so much wrong to be
righted. There is so much misery to be minis-
tered to. There is so much sin to be driven out.
There is so much hunger to be fed. There is so
much nakedness to be clothed. You warming
yourself? The Church of Christ stands beside
your comfortable place now and points out the
way. You are needed to help make a better city,
and a better country, and a better world, and
no man has much time to spare, or much fuel
that can be afforded on so little a task as merely
to keep himself warm.

FOR OTHERS

FOR OTHERS

"For their sakes I sanctify myself."—*John 17. 19.*

I COUNT that text one of the chief sentences
of all the world's story. There occur, here and
there through human history, outstanding sentences which seem to epitomize dominant facts
and motives of life. Such words have not infre-
quently come from dying patriots, or from mar-
tyrs facing hardest death; towering souls who
have set eternal and cosmopolitan truth in phrase
to ring down the ages. Jesus Christ was wording
the very divinest and best of His heart and soul
all through this wonderful seventeenth chapter
of John, as He poured out His yearnings in
prayer. Amid it all (and this by many is called
the most remarkable chapter in the Bible) there
is no passage that seems to give expression to His
dedication of purpose and ministry, as does this
text, when He seems to stand tip-toe in the consciousness of His divinity, and looking far down
the streaming centuries to note the multitude
who would need help in every phase life could
know, He declares, "For their sakes." For
those poor millions! For those ignorant hosts!
For those worn multitudes! For those who are
weary and heavy laden! For those sorrowing

ones! For those who die! For those who fight
fierce temptations! For those who struggle to
know better life! Only God can know what He
saw when He said it, but all of us who have
lived far on down the ranks since His day, know
a bit He saw; and know what He sees now, and
pray for strength to stand with Him and look
steadfastly at what there is to be seen in need
to-day. "For their sakes I sanctify myself."
Somehow, under inspiration of such unqualified
dedication as that to whatever needed Him, I
believe we who call ourselves Christians this
hard but opportune day, must find our challenging program.

Jesus Christ has not failed. He has never fled
a single field, nor changed a single purpose. The
triumph of our Captain means the dominance of
His purpose, and we who claim to be His, must
show our faith in His plan. If ever you did try
to espouse Christianity with a little selfish ideal,
this day will spoil all that for you. Christianity
will destroy your ease. It is no recreation program. It was not designed for comfort. It
will subscribe your time and substance. It en-
lists your sacrifice. It points to the cross. It
has adopted a program worth doing and seeks
not to lure folks to it by any baited ease. When
we wanted men to go to war, and run breast forward into battle where steel flew in cruel peril,
we frankly told men what we wanted, and men

came because the call was big enough to enlist
them. It is not promise of ease that wins espousal of brave souls. Christianity arises now
as always calling for sacrifice. Calling for hearts
keen enough to feel the hurting wrongs mankind
is suffering. Calling for eyes keen enough to see
the things which spoil comfort. But it calls with
heroic possibilities that should find response in
the heart of any man or woman who looks on life
as a task rather than a mere existence.

"O God! I cried, why may I not forget?
These halt and hurt in life's hard battle throng me yet.
Am I their keeper? Only I—to bear
This constant burden of their grief and care?
Why must I suffer for the other's sin?
Would that my eyes had never opened been!
And the thorn-crowned and patient One
Replied, 'They thronged Me too. I have seen.'

"Thy other children go at will, I said protesting still;
They go unheeding. But these sick and sad,
These blind and orphan, yea, and those that sin,
Drag at my heart. For them I serve and groan—
Why is it? Let me rest, Lord. I have tried.
He turned and looked at me and said,
'But I have died.'

"But, Lord, this ceaseless travail of my soul,
This stress! This often fruitless toil!
These souls to win!
They are not mine. I brought not forth this host
Of needy creatures, struggling, tempest-tossed,
They are not mine.
He looked at them, the look of One Divine,
He turned and looked at me.
'But they are mine.'

"O God! I said, I understand at last.
Forgive, and henceforth I will bond-slave be
To the least, weakest, vilest ones.
I would no more be free.
He smiled and said, 'It is to Me.' "

O God! help me to preach this hour the thing I
know is the passion of Thine Own heart, and
which should leap to a consuming flame in all
our souls. This is distinctly Christianity. It
cannot look complacently upon any type of need.
It is keyed even to a much higher program than
that, and has been leading the world in its pio-
neering in service, as it has responded even to
the point of genuine sacrifice. So faithful, thank
God, has been her work thus far, that her great
campaigns for missions, as they have measured
devotion against the deep sorrows of heathenism,
have at last gotten a place in national consciousness, until now one section in the covenant of the
League of Nations deals with the duties of the
nations toward the backward and untutored
nations of mankind. What is that but the missionary program become a political fact among
the nations? This is the distinguishment of
Christianity always, and he who espouses it must
find himself linked at once with the campaign
for world-redemption. You will find this fact
dominant in every outstanding character the
church has ever produced. It was this which
transformed a Jew, a Pharisee of the Pharisees;

proud, clannish, jealous of his whole racial distinction, into a Christian, humble and seeking to serve others. Saul became Paul, and the difference between the two men was exactly expressed in our text, and he who had been a mean persecutor became a solicitous servant saying, "I am debtor! I am debtor," and went about his life to the end, seeking by tireless earnestness to discharge his obligation. Under leadership of such a conviction that man arose on the world to become a figure so large that only Jesus Christ surpasses him in influence upon mankind. But even Paul would have gone down in death and been buried in the oblivion of the multitude, had he not caught the genius of service in his life. He saved his life by giving it. This is the genius of a life worth while, to discover that it can never discharge its obligation to the world that needs every man's best laid upon its great altar to make the whole world go heavenward, until it has caught the spirit of genuine consecration for others. Any man anywhere who catches step with this fine truth will march straight into the world's heart and revive it. I know no greater truth to challenge this strong day of ours with than this. Thank God for the men and women who do live it. God help all the rest of us to gather courage to endorse it. "For their sakes I sanctify myself." What a truth that is to appeal to strong men with. The consciousness of strength is at once a liability. Paul worked out, I am sure, as effectual and consistent a model of Christian activity as has ever been accomplished by a man. He went to Rome with his message. He was a hated and despised Jew, but that never hindered the deliverance of his message. He waded through sufferings, and mobs, and shipwreck, and blood. "Listen, Rome! I have a word for you. You are much used to the bringing from far of gifts for your treasury. You sit proud on your seven hills. Your converging roads have been beaten hard by trains of treasure brought to your extravagant call. Great armies of men have laid their gold, their manhood, their lives at your feet. I come to take the responsibility of saying a new thing to you. Thus far you have known life merely as receptive. You have had ushers merely to show the treasure bearers where to pour out their gold. Rome, you have an absolutely false view of life. You don't know me, but I come to declare heaven's fundamentals to you in terms of Jesus. You are great to be of service. Your strength is your debt. You are obligated for every treasure you hold. Wealth is not an asset, it is a liability." Some of those proud old Romans laughed at such a message from such a source. "Who is this prisoner philosopher-religionist who talks so? What do we care about the need of others. Let them crawl before us here. Let them bring

tribute. We have the mailed fist. We have their
necks lashed to our chariot wheels." But to-day
as you dig amid the tumbled ruins of that old
Rome, and the many ruins of the past it repre-
sents, you will come to appreciate the ever growing power of the message of the Gospel, and that
as surely as God's hand is on this world's life,
men are coming to know that the strength of the
world must carry its obligations. Power was not
granted you to make you a mere collector of
revenues, but rather to endow you with obligation. Power is debt. Every power is a liability.
Hard lesson that to learn. If we are smart, or
cultured, or rich, or endowed with any command-
ing talent, it seems so easy to give it a selfish
coinage. We plume ourselves in our strength,
and level a tax on the world for it. The temptation of power has always been to select a strate-
gic place, and charge the world toll. "Pay me!
Pay me! I am entitled to the tribute of a world
that should count itself fortunate that I am here.
The world should recognize me." Thus saith the
strong man, as he sets himself up for toll. It is
so easy for strength to become egotistical.
Goethe's extreme egotism, which I used to believe
was a mere heathen spot that at times found expression in his sayings, but which I believe now,
was developed into a consuming power of Germany at her worst, and became at last the very
devouring judgment upon them; Goethe's ego-

tism found expression once in a bold declaration
as he drew himself to confident proportions to
say, "The man who has life in him, feels himself
to be here for his own sake, and not for the sake
of the public." That is the wreck of power, the
prostitution of endowment. He who squanders
entrusted strength in selfishness, shall reap the
reward of an outraged world. A man has not
begun to breathe the real sense of power until
he catches the appreciation of an overpowering
moral indebtedness. His greatness has not taken
safe root until it recognizes that in itself is
the power to help and better the world. A contribution is asked of us for the invisible interests
of the universe. We are here charged to do
something for the betterment of the world. We
are not here to collect our dues. We are
here to pay our bills. That concerns me much.
All humanity has a claim on me. I cannot shake
it off. "No man liveth to himself," and God
means that the real conviction of that fact shall
work itself out in the solicitation from each of
us, "Then, to whom do I live?" Maybe God gets
a strange hearing when cannon roar and the
very foundations of government are broken up,
and the basic rocks of society seem to be shaken
in the swelling thereof. It is certain there is a
listening attitude to-day on the part of much in
the world that only a short gone yesterday
seemed stone-deaf to every voice of altruism. Let

strong men hear this word. Let rich men hear
it. Let cultured folks appreciate it. Let talented
lives accept it. Let all those who sit in ease, and
dare to enjoy comforts which are brought them
in hands hard worked, hear it. This is not a
cry for poverty. We have as a world grown
used to the sacrifices the poor and the weak have
had to make, for shamefully much of the progress of the world has been made at the price of
sacrifice by the weak. The strong must now
catch this call. Hear Jesus in the consciousness of the very highest of His strength, "For
their sakes I sanctify myself." Yea, Lord, we
hear you! We understand you too. We live
when the reflected implication in it to us comes
clothed in whole nations and races in need! We
live when our faith in Thee stands challenged
by the greatest privilege of service that has ever
spread itself before Thy Church! We live when
heathenism is opening every long-locked door,
and actually begging us in haste to come! We
live when exhausted, war-broken civilization is
asking for the message of human cooperation and
brotherhood! Lord God of Hosts! help, that
none of us shall falter now! Help us to stand
up and look straight into the task now. We
must not prove unworthy the price that has been
paid for our living. It is actually more difficult to live now in a manner that will justify
our inheritance of this great blood-bought hour,

than it was for the noble men who went out and died to bring it in.

"After actual centuries of struggle for the so-called rights of equality, there is some reason now to believe that through the great crimson gates leading out from bleeding fields of battle where unusual victories were won, mankind is now entering upon the struggle for the rights of inequality." Somewhat thus one of our great Americans spoke recently to the students of a law school. That is the philosophy of Christianity, as socially exceeding the high philosophy and purpose of democracy. Democracy is the rights of equality. Christianity recognizes the debt of the strong. After all I have gotten nothing very great when I have gotten my rights. I want my rights, and I want others to have theirs. But I ask for a much larger life in this world than that of merely clipping my coupons. I want to put something in too. O, for that truth to break out like a passion among us. There are few, if there are any, more terrible pictures Jesus ever drew, than the one He left us about a man who was absolutely unable to feel this great obligation. The man's name was Dives. He had a constant opportunity to understand the sense of his debt, by the delegated beggar who sat at his gate, and yet was not so much as even noticed, save by the dogs, and even the dogs licked his sores. But Dives came out of his great house,

through multitudes of good bargains, and never
so much as knew there was a beggar inside his
horizon. I am Dives! See me! So walked care-
lessly the rich man. And Jesus says here, that in
the next world Dives had to remember what he
forgot here. The cutting pain for him is that all
the time his opportunity sat right at his gate.
He had to step over it. But he never saw it.
Every ounce of extra strength you have, you are
duty bound to find out where you can best invest
it for good. Every power you possess is im-
paired if it misses the element of ministry. The
world is creditor, not you. "You are not your
own." "No man liveth to himself." "I am debtor
to the Jew, and to the Gentile." "For their
sakes I sanctify myself." Surely such scripture
is not obscure in its meaning. But we spend ourselves upon ourselves. If once the great work of
lifting this world would become the purpose of
the strong, if we could awaken the active interest
of all those who have strength commensurate to
the task, we would feel the quick thrill of ad-
vance and this old world would leap heavenward
in mighty bounds.

The most troubling thing at the minds of men
now is the complicated social question. It has
always been a troubler. But, under the loosen-
ing of great democratic ideals there has appeared
an unusual strengthening to the submerged
rights of the multitude. The whole social trouble

of the world has arisen because one section of
society has repudiated its debt to the other. Society can never find a peace founded on classes.
The idea of classes is a certain disturber of the
peace. The contention and determination of the
mad Bolshevist is simply to turn society upside
down. He keeps the classes. He only proposes
an inverted autocracy. He would put the office-
force at the bench and bring bench-workers into
the office. I saw some time ago a searching picture of the social conditions in Europe. It represented a great ball-room, where luxury was in
full swing of careless enjoyment of its own pleasures. The floor of the dance hall was upheld by
strong hands and brawny shoulders. Suddenly
at one place in the floor a clenched hard fist had
broken up through, and consternation spread
throughout the hall because of it. There can
never be any success or peace won in society
through the idea of stratified classes. Society
will never be regulated horizontally in social
strata. All social troubles have arisen for the
reason that the so-called upper class don't appreciate the honor and claim of the lower side, and
the lower side despises the boast and claim of the
upper side. Out of this unjust condition much of
the strength of the world has interpreted its contribution to the good of the whole, as a charity
and a benevolence. The great obligation can
never be discharged on that basis. You cannot

save the world as a charity. The unavoidable
call of the world's needy life is an obligation. It
is a debt. I have been unfolding before my soul
the appeals of a world's need. I have charts and
charts. I have been counting what nations and
races need. I have been summing up the call
from our own nation's frontiers. I have been
looking squarely at the great festering spots in
the great cities. My soul burns with all the
pressing appeals. All ignorance, and stupidity,
and degradation, are world claims on those who
are above them. That principle stands clear in
this great Book of God. The obligation of power
is to weakness. Such a sense of obligation in-
heres in the organic connection of things.

"Were ye of the seekers,
    Ye fallen, ye merged in the mire,
When ye clutched so and stumbled and stiffled,
    Were ye led by desire,
God's angel of longing whose task is
    To set souls afire?

"Too feeble the flame of your burning!
    Was passion so pale,
Ye could drown it in draughts for the body,
Could nothing avail to fire you to mightily conquer,
    Or mightily fail?

"Nay truly, God's angel of longing
    Who sets souls afire,
Must chafe when the snatched spark of heaven,
    Falls so in the mire,
To sputter in pitiful sinning,
    And weakly expire."

The one who stands must see the one who falls. "For their sakes! For their sakes!" We were not made strong for extravagance. Think what the world had had, if many of those who to-day stand great, because they were good servants, had dared to consume themselves. Let Paul go self-consumed out of the world. What would the world have missed had he not seen clearly his obligation? He had a fine intellect. He was a trained scholar. Let him go back home and build about him in Tarsus a place of personal pleasure. He was strong enough to have easily lured luxury his way. Think what he might have escaped too. He could doubtless have lived on to a comfortable old age, and died in a good bed, pillowed in ease, surrounded by servants to fan into his failing lungs their last panting breath. But let me see the list of all those prominent people of Tarsus who did do that. Surely there are famous ones there. Get me the city directory of Tarsus, or of any other city, that will show me those famous ones who have steered clear of hardship and sat in cushioned comfort of selfish ease. They are all forgotten. Why should we remember them? Paul could have missed the prison and the stocks and the stinging whip-cords. He could have escaped the mob in Jerusalem. He needed not to have endured the shipwreck at Malta. He could have slipped the chains and prison at Rome. He was

not compelled to bend over the blood-smeared
block. "Go home to ease, Paul! Go sit down to
your comfort! I know you are strong, and your
great endeavor will send a thrill throughout the
world for centuries. But it will cost you dearly,
Paul! It will cut your very soul! Go home to
Tarsus, and sit down quietly and write philosophy! Why make a fool of yourself and be
hounded by hatred and killed at last as a crim-
inal!" So spoke the wisdom of comfort. But
Paul, who might have been a lazy forgotten
Rabbi, and been buried in the oblivion of all those
other citizens of Tarsus, made the brave choice,
and turning his life in service to others for
Christ's sake, marched straight to its great end,
and died gloriously for a cause, rather than as a
mere worn-out human machine, and wrote the
only name that Tarsus has given the world, and
wrote it at the top. That was what Jesus was
trying to say to active conviction in the lives of
men, when He gave us the words of His own
dedication in our text. The responsibility of
ability is ringing in our ears to-day. Endowment means service. You are all men. You must
pay up. This is the high sense of Christian obligation. He who wears the name Christian cannot go feelingless and deaf and sightless through
a world like this in which we live. Walking
along our wretched streets where poverty
crouches in suffering, the beggar may not by law

be allowed to stop you, but every crumbling
shanty and bare window calls to you. Go among
the ignorant, and the very silence of their ignorance drives your obligation into your deepest
heart. Stagger down the filthy avenues of the
unmentionable sorrow. The wretched impurity
that glares at you from the windows of nameless
grief, don't ask you for virtue in so many words,
but you can't be a Christian if out of every robbed
face and vacant eye, there be not an appeal to
you for help. Go stumbling along the blasted
broken roads of ruined France, and Belgium, and
Serbia, and Armenia, and Poland. Look into the
gaunt faces there. Look into the pitiful eyes of
little children whose joys have been stolen and
from whose wasted faces all smiles seem forever
rubbed away. Open your eyes to your day, and
you will see that you cannot be a Christian now
unless you have caught this passion of Jesus.
"For their sakes! For their sakes!" This is the
call of our opportunity. I know it means struggle severe. But when once the full sense of it
has gripped our appreciation we will never find
ease any other where than in the performance of
our duty.

THE BATTLE OF THE BARNS

THE BATTLE OF THE BARNS

"He said" . . . "But God said."—*Luke 12. 18-20.*

THE familiar parable from which I have taken
these two terse but significant and opposing
phrases has always been one of the most interesting of all the parables of Jesus. It presents such
complex interest. You can see so very far along
the problematic ways of men. Our Lord was putting in an easily told story the deepest philosophy of life. A certain rich man had a fertile
farm. He had made it pay him continuous dividends, and had stored up much of his extra
bounty. The crops one year were unusually good.
As he saw them assured, he realized the embarrassment which would be his if he had to simply
pile the abundant grain outside, with no shelter,
when there were so many people about who had
no grain to store. He was clearly troubled. All
his barns were full of the abundant crops of
years before, which he could not consume, and
which he had not been compelled to sell. There
were, to be sure, many empty bins about the country that might have been used. There were hungry and poor folks who could have housed a great
amount of the embarrassment. But he saw only
his crop and the fact that his bins were full.

The interpretation of all crops, and the clearing house of all disposals to which he was partner, was his own interest. His bins were full. It was not satisfaction. It was problematic. It always is. He shaped all his policy before his own bins. That is a narrow threshold whereon to map out a program for life. But it is not a rare place to do it. So he sat down on the threshold of his bulging bins, and facing the rich nodding crops that were ripening in his fields, began to draw some pretentious plans for additional barns. He decided, as he figured thus by himself, that if he was really to become the man he could be, he should have far greater barns than these full bins he now possessed. So he tore up the first plans he had in mind, the mere building of additional room, and said, "This I will do, I will pull these down and build greater." Now in itself there is nothing wrong in that, and the pity of it all lies in the hard fact that had he taken a greater view of what he possessed he would have made his increasing fortune a blessing to all around him, as well as a delight to his own soul. For he who gets no more out of riches than riches is still a poor man, little matter how large his bins. This man was interpreting the bounty of the earth in his own bins. He got the process backwards. I feel very sure that God would have been glad for him to have had larger barns and full barns too. It is not the size of a man's bins that troubles the administration of providence. It is such an easy thing for a man to try to measure all the things he can get in this world by his own bins. He knows the cubic measure of prosperity, and the only thing he knows to do when that measure is exhausted is to build larger. Now the size of the barns, after all, is of no concern in the real fact which enters here. The trouble in the case of this much prospered man is, that he should be so careless in his blessings as to think that he could build barns that would hold for him far more than he had any need of, and yet that he might hold in the selfish greed of himself. What a fine thing this man, whom Christ boldly called a fool, could have done for himself and all the ages to come, had he been big enough to arise before his prosperity and say, "Who can measure the real goodness of God? I will treasure it and seek to interpret it for His Name's sake." But that was not his purpose at all. "And he said . . . But God said," and those are the front line trenches in this battle of the barns, fought out then in the tragic results Jesus has told us of, and fought out many, many times since when selfishness has reared itself against God. "He said." That is this determined rich man "digging in," as the boys from the lines used to say. "But God said." That is the destruction of those human trenches, as with one mighty bomb, for God's contradic-

tion is infinitely more powerful than all the purposes man can build.

To my mind this has drawn a clearer out-
line of a man's need of the appreciation of more
than himself in order to interpret even his own
life, than any other incident recorded in the
Book. It is, merely in story form, the actual history of a great many lives in this world. If it
comes in square collision with us now, may God
help us always to interpret constructively
whatever of opposition He may have to throw
against our plans. I received a letter one day
from a noble father whose son had by a great mistake fallen into the hands of the law. The father
was a lawyer and he asked me to go to the prison
and see his boy and do all I could so he would
interpret his punishment constructively. God's
relationship to us is always constructive in purpose. We may not see it always. When barns
fall down and our little plans are torn to pieces
in our hands by death we do not see very
well. But I have a faith in God, that could
not interpret His opposition any other way than
constructive. Whenever I walk boldly into His
bounty with no other sense of it than the mere
size of my bin, then my bin will doubtless feel
the hand of God laid upon it, and I shall be left
ere long, with what bin I had in ruin and the
larger bin I had planned to build, unbuilt, because the mistake of my life was that I saw

nothing more in my grain-filled fields than a hoarding chance for myself.

"And he said." Let us sit square before that entry now, and see what we can make out of life with it, as far as God will let us go, for God will be sure to stop that fact sooner or later in every one of us. Set it all down now. I said this, and I said that. Bring out that fortune you have so planfully laid out to make, and maybe you have made much of it too thus far. You will be tempted to plume yourself a bit, as you pour the glittering gold you have gathered through your fingers that have possessed it, or as you pile your papers for houses and lands, beside your lathe-printed bonds. Or, you who have no gold and stocks, it is no sure sign of your sanctification that you have no fortune. Your purpose may have been just as self-centered, may have been more so. Selfishness can still be just as fatal, even when it has no dividends in stock to declare. It is not so much a question of the amount a man's barns may be able to hold, or whether or no he has been able to get built the sized bins he had planned; it is altogether a question as to whether or no he himself stood at the door of his barns, whatever their capacity, and left God out of the reckoning of his harvests. Life may so very easily become a thing of small horizons. It may easily be shut up in a little old barn. Or for that matter in a big old barn. Make thou sure it

is not the size of the barn that counts. It is the
barniness of the barn. It is shutting the soul up.
Life comes so seriously easy to all of us to be
but a narrow treasure. Why should I trouble
my head and heart with all these distracting
things of others? Only the other day a fine young
fellow, who for some time now and in most efficient manner, has been throwing his enthusiasm
into the great struggle for righteousness in encouraging manner, came to me and said that he
had lost interest in such things now, and henceforth he was not going to worry his heart over
it all. His bins are full already, and business
already is showing him a certain overflow, and
he is sitting now on the threshold of his bulging
success, drawing larger plans in selfish absorbing interest. I am afraid for that man. "Why
should I, I, I." "I will build my own barns
larger."

The staggering shock of the war we thought
would startle many to a better sense of life. And
we did look steadily at life, for almost five
slaughtering years, shrouded in death. So many
people were just alive. It is so fatal to life to
be merely alive. Enough to eat. Plenty of air
to breathe. A comfortable bed for rest. Bins all
full. Life as mere living is sufficient. That had
grown to be a human liability. Our civilization
has been haunted by it. You were infected with
the danger. We were about ready to plan per-

manent abodes right here. We were so sure of
our barns. They were so well filled. We did not
calculate on anything else that might come. This
life is its own interpretation. Our reason, our
imagination, our pleasure, were satisfied. What
more could we need than to be simply alive?
This was the soothing charm that ringed us
round. We worked some, but work has lost so
much of its drudgery. We talked, we played,
we laughed, we sang. We could scarce believe
that each generation, even our very own, must
pass away, and that we too one day must actually grow dull to life and fatigued, and at last
fall fatally ill and come staggering up to look
death in the face. Death itself we had doctored
into a helpless sort of a stupor, and we would
soothe it down with narcotics and slip through
the portals where pain had sat watching before
our graves in a senseless sort of a way. "And
we said! And we said." Suddenly the most
awful war the world has ever dreamed of broke
upon us and all our plans went down in a crash,
and great mad death ran rampant everywhere.
Death everywhere, and by every means. Only it
seemed forever arm-locked with big strong youth.
And youth conquered it too. Our men learned
how to die. They never flinched. They looked
it straight in the face. They incorporated it
into their plans. It broke no plan or purpose for
them. What I am trying to say to you in this great

fact that has come scarce recognized trampling
up out of the reddened fields of war, is this very
same thing we started in merest personal terms
with, which has run now to nations and humanity
as a whole and must use large figures with which
to demonstrate. This whole world of ours has
been moving along in so self-sufficient a manner,
for so long, that the ordinary attitude of many
folks toward God has been such as would be expressed only as a necessity. You will remember
how keenly Shakespeare has put the fact in
Henry V, when the hostess was telling of the
death of Falstaff. "A' cried out, God! God! God!
three or four times. Now I, to comfort him, bade
him he should not think of God. I hoped there
was no no need to trouble himself with any such
thoughts yet." No need yet. It was not a question of need, but only a question of calling God
too soon. As if God were a mere necessity which
all good sense counseled avoiding as long as possible. The Battle of the Barns, the very same old
conflict where the selfish plan of life is only to be
overcome when the divine plan arises to drive it
out.

"But God said." We are seeing here the largest truth of life written by Christ in familiar
terms upon a short biography of a man who shut
God out of his plans, made vast gains, but lost
his soul. This man had said his say, "but God
said." What a tremendous entry that, to thrust

abruptly thus into the selfish story of any man's
life. It is so easy to become enamored of barns,
and to set the figures of life all in the cheap
terms of our crops. And barns and crops don't
mean merely old weather-beaten shanties filled
with corn. They may be granite blocks and
bags of gold. The fault here is not in the poor
nature of barns and crops, but lies rather in the
fact that the spiritual considerations of loyalty
and duty and surrender to God are wholly set
aside, and if so, it matters little what it may have
been done for, barns and corn are as good as
anything. I speak carefully, and choose my
words when I say, that whenever our lives are
made to revolve around self, God simply must
break those plans down. I have such absolute
faith in my God over me, that I will not stagger
in my belief in Him even when He shatters all
my fondest hopes to the ground. If the barns
of my purpose are tumbled about my head, I
shall still gather confidence in His higher purpose. One afternoon in a large hospital in Ban-
gour in Scotland I met a very attractive young
soldier well on the the way to recovery, who had
suffered a most serious wound. He had been
struck in seven places by a bursting shrapnel.
He was so severely hit that he lay down on the
kindly ground to die. He told me he had no
thought or intention ever to try to rise again.
His life was ebbing away from every gaping

wound. An officer came by and spoke kindly to
him and told him to get up and he would help
him seek some aid. The poor struck fellow looked
up and said, "Officer, I am here to die. Leave me
alone now, and it will soon be done." The officer
urged him to come along. I shall never forget
how the lad looked when he said to me, "Sir,
for the first time in all my life I refused to obey
orders, and said to my officer, 'I will lie here and
die.' " Then the officer bent over him and said,
"Now, sir, I am going to be cruel but kind. I
command you to get up and come with me."
The poor hurt fellow began to try to struggle to
his feet, and the officer helped him, and carried
and dragged him in at last to the first line dressing station, where he received first aid and was
hurried on to the clearing station, where the officer sought him out again just as he was ready to
start for "Blighty," as the British troops call
home, and bending over the sufferer, he asked
solicitously, "Will you forgive me, Tommy, for
my kind cruelty?" When I saw that boy and got
the story out of his thankful heart as he was well
on the way to complete recovery, the kindness of
what seemed cruel opposition to his own wishes
was the one outstanding memory he had of it
all. "There's a kindness in God's justice." "But
God said," not simply to bring on opposition to
the plans I have set up. Surely none of us are
going to carry so cramped an idea of our Master's

purpose to believe that He is working in our lives to disappoint our hopes. Can we not arise to believe, and believing to claim the fact that His opposition will prove the means of delivering us from unsuspected and even almost unbelievable evil which lurks in our own plans? He does not intend to cross our best energies. He seeks ever to better them by turning them to higher purposes than those which we, sitting alone on the small doorsteps of our little barns, would ever plan out. It is so very easy to become enamored of our barns. I do not claim to know how this difficult day of ours, in which the whole world seems caught in the collapse of much we have all held dear, can come to the help we need. I can hear the roar of the tumbling barns. There is yet clear before my memory the confident plans we had made for the larger barns we were so sure we would build. They were God-careless barns too. The world had been inclined to forget God in its plans. The utterly misdirected leadership of materialism had made Germany so self-centered that it saw only German barns. I am not saying that Germany was the lone offender in this. I am saying, however, that her dominant philosophy and plans were outstandingly materialistic. I am saying that the whole world was careless on its divine side. We were enamored of our fields. We were confident of our factories. We were sure of our science. We were comfort-

able in our riches. We were self-centered because we were self-trusting. But our barns are
down. It seemed for a while that the heavens
were falling. But they were not. We were too close
to our barns, that was all. We need now, with the
dust of our tumbled barns rubbed from our eyes,
to help the coming generation shake itself free
from all this collapsed materialism, and pluck
up the courage, and the foresight, and the noble
daring, and go straight about it and bring God
into the life of our day. Let us read clearly the
real big facts that underlie this Battle of the
Barns, this materialistic course of life. Already the world should have known this truth
from its former experience. For this is not new
teaching, but only a modern rendering of the old
fact. Up till this day we call ours, the bloodiest
page that was ever written on the scroll of history was written by poor misguided France in
a strange day of her experience. She struck her
pen in the blood of her best sons and daughters
and scrawled a hideous message when she went
stumbling through the tragedy of the French
Revolution. What did that tragic thing? Atheism did it! Bold, blatant atheism. They made
national declaration against God, "There is no
God!" They said! They said! They enthroned
Reason. They lifted a fair faced harlot from the
streets of Paris and throned her high as "The
Goddess of Reason." She died later in an insane

hospital, without reason or friends or money. What did all this? Atheism did it. Upon the world's troubled pages again has been written, and written more bloody than any other ever has been, the story of a crossed purpose. We have scarce recovered ourselves enough to contemplate what has been done, but we are sure what caused the collapse. Materialism did it. What is materialism? It is the modern and scientific way of spelling atheism. It is the very same tragedy again. The war is a colossal danger-signal, set to glow so terribly, that no future generation shall ever be able to forget, what we have found so fatal in forgetting, namely, that we cannot leave God out of life. A remarkable poster was posted in large type all over England during the war. I copied it in my note book with profound interest. It was the utterance and careful message of an influential man and soldier. It read as follows: "I fear that even yet too many of us are putting an undue amount of trust in chariots and horses. We may confidently rely upon our soldiers and sailors fighting bravely. We may count upon their having abundant ammunition. But we must not stop at that. A serious determination on the part of the nation to seek and deserve divine help would, we may hope, enable us to take a true perspective of this war, and it would undoubtedly furnish valuable help to our gallant soldiers and sailors at the

front." Signed, General Sir W. Robertson. I
am sure, my Christian friends, we must come out
of this hard day of ours, bathed in a new sense
of our need of God. "But God said! But God
said!" You men and women, who up till now
have been sitting confident in the mere fact of
full barns and well drawn plans for larger ones,
to hold the larger yields of what you feel sure
are richer years ahead, I would call to you to save
you from your barns. There are in life great
unselfish ideals which must enlist you. They
may even strain you to the point of suffering, but
they will save you at last above the wreckage of
all your barns and bins. It must be true, that
out of the old selfish ideals of life, our world
must come on into a newer and higher and
diviner ideal. For the true vision of God that
must lie beyond and above the life of to-day, we
have been coming on through the sorrows of the
world suffering of the scarce closed yesterday.
The loss and rejection of that vision in the more
careless days of our wealth is that which has
brought us into our prostration. O God! open
these eyes of ours! Help us to see clearly out
of the rolling dust of our tumbled and tumbling
barns. We want life! Right life! "And he said!
But God said!" Help us to hear clearly what
Thou hast to say to us, in order that we may say
also Thy will. "Our wills are ours, to make them
thine." The Battle of the Barns.

THE LONENESS OF LIFE

THE LONENESS OF LIFE

"Behold, we knew not this man."—*Prov. 24. 12.*

I USE this text in the revised version, because the old version does not make its meaning clear, stating only, "Behold, we knew it not." I seek a passage that will declare the fact we all realize so very well, that we are unknown, that conscious loneness of life which at times almost haunts us, and yet defies every effort we may make to drive it away. To me this presents one of the most interesting phases of human personality, and carries a far-cry that I am sure is a prophet in meaning. What soul do you know? Who has anyone ever known? Does anyone in all the world really know you? There lies in there the most fascinating mystery human life holds, and I want to pursue it for a while now because I know there is religious meaning in it. Mystery is always fascinating. Just why that is true I am not able to say, but I am sure there is universal fascination in the mere fact of mystery. The house on your street where the blinds are always drawn, you feel at times you simply must look into, and the next door where all the curtains are up day and night, you don't even glance toward. Mystery whets curiosity. When

191

you drape personality in mystery you have added its greatest interest. The keen fact declared in this old proverb is the matter we have always known about ourselves, and in a manner prided ourselves upon it, as our safe defense, with which we could sit secure even in a crowd. We know no one really knows about us, but we have not allowed that fact to be an unbreakable fact of all people.

I propose now to interpret this isolation of life as a positive testimony reserved to the need of the soul for God. Man cannot survive loneness, and yet, without God, we can but stumble along, and suffer the pang of the consciousness of being unknown. There is a sacred sanctum, a Holy of Holies in every heart into which even the nearest friend cannot enter. No matter now how close friendship may come in this world, and thank God it can at times come very close, but no two lives can get inside each other. In every heart remains that unmolested area. The poet wrote a usable couplet, which has been worn out for a certain period of life, when folks turn more easily to rhyme than to poetry. It was about two lives with but a single thought, and two hearts beating as one. But it is only a short step to the discovery of the difference between poetry and fact, as folks settle down to the appreciation that the song of two hearts must forever be a duet. There remain secret corners in our deepest hearts to

which no one can ever enter. The increasingly
strange thing about this is that we all long for
some one to enter into this loneness. We have all
felt it often and at times would tear our very
hearts asunder and lay open the way. O come
in! Come in to me. And yet they have not come.
They could not come. We could not let them in.

Up to this seeming discrepancy in our lives,
which I am sure I have poorly thus sketched to
you, but of the fact of which I know your personal knowledge in your own case will supple-
ment my failure to describe, I wish now to declare my belief that this is one of God's own ways
of claiming His own, and of reserving the right
divine to every soul. My contention is, that this
yearning for sympathy and intimate acquaint-
ance, which human hearts cannot fulfill, is one of
the most forceful arguments for God. There
has never been a human soul that has been able
to escape this compelling fact. Men have been
able to build up great arguments to defend themselves in unbelief, but their own inmost souls
have still cried for the living God. The man
who goes against God must go trampling over
the very deepest fact of his own consciousness.

> "In the sea of life enisled,
>   With echoing straits between us thrown,
> Dotting the shoreless watery wild,
>   We mortal millions live alone.
> The islands feel the enclasping flow,
> And then their endless bounds they know."

Something there is for every one of us in each
joy as in each sorrow which no one can share.
We go pushing our way amid the crowding popu-
lace, conscious that unbreakable secrets crouch
behind our sealed lips. Some one of the philoso-
phers has observed that everyone has much in
common, and when you know well one man you
know well all men, but that the commonest thing
which characterizes all men is that we are all
isolated and alone. You are much more than a
mere collection of the common passions that,
bundled together in a bit of mortal casement, go
to make up a human figure. Humanity is not
an assembled machine. We have developed great
efficiency in manufacturing machinery these days
from standardized parts, and selecting a certain
number of bolts and screws and bars and wheels
from the regular sorted up stock piles, can assem-
ble identical machines, every part of which is a
mere selection from a thousand more exactly
like it waiting to be hurled into some collection,
sure to be the very same sort when assembled. Man is not an assembled mortality,
though the physiologist can by knowing some
dead body know somewhat of my anatomy. Beyond you, and within you there is that distin-
guishing inner life, whose current we at times
detect, but which flows on in solitary stillness.
The very best friendships cannot get inside
that fact. Mr. Wordsworth was feeling about

in this same strange region of the soul when he
wrote,

"To friendship let him turn
For succor; but perhaps he sits alone,
On stormy waters, tossed in a little boat,
That holds but him, and can contain no more."

Whatever else you may have caught at from
this fact of loneliness, I wish to press it as a dis-
tinct testimony to the significance and sacredness
of each individual life. I want you to be saved
from that rampant scientific tendency of our day,
of the classification of the species, and to fix
your attention upon the fact that above all else
you are a peculiar personality, and attendant on
that is the further truth that the inner sanctum
of your heart, while you yearn for it to be occupied, even you cannot open it to let anyone in.
I remember an interesting incident that happened in the court house where I once lived. The
newly elected county clerk came into his office
and the first night closed the great safe and
locked it, only to find that he had locked in the
new combination, and no one knew what it was.
They greatly desired some one to get into that
safe, but could not tell anyone how to do it. They
finally imported an expert, a man from the factory where the vault had been made, and after
great effort they with slight injury broke in. We
know something of each other's outward appear-
ance. We can recognize as acquaintances some

of the folks we meet oftenest. We even at times become so expert as to detect voices, or the peculiar footfalls of their walk across the floor. There are some folks who naturally live such open, glad, welcome lives, they are fairly thronged with lovers, and everybody seems to know them. There are others who on certain days are at home to a few callers at specified hours. There are others we do not remember ever having seen with a hint of welcome evident. Yet often the very life with whom we had thought we were best acquainted, unexpectedly showed us a closed room, or lifted a heretofore close-drawn curtain and revealed a nature we had never once dreamed of there. Sit down some time and take an invoice of all those racing thoughts that chased each other only the day before through your vigorous brain, and then strike out those that actually became known to anybody on earth and you will be amazed at the disclosure of how absolutely alone you are living, even in the ordinary. Some hideous dream went trampling through your sleeping hours. From whence it could have arisen in your soul's depths you shudder to think. But with a startle as you awoke in terror you profoundly thanked God it was a dream, and would never tell anyone you even dreamed such a thing. All this is a breaking to consciousness of the fact that every one of us is living a life above depths we cannot reveal. All this is just as true from the angle of joy as it is from that of distress. The joy of pure love; the joy of the mother in the dawning life of her child; the delight of the student who catches the first flash of the long sought truth; the joy of the rescuer of precious lives from the grip of sin; the peace of the martyr, who sees through the leaping flame the truth secure which he had a thousand times rather die possessing than to live surrendering. In some form this has come upon you when your biggest self was in the throes of some great struggle, and feeling about for words you could find none, for we have no language for such moments, and as the tears sprang to your eyes you said, "I cannot tell you! I cannot speak!"

O this great big secret self I have! What is it for anyhow? It is forever misunderstood. Holding me in its spell I easily misunderstand others. What can I do for it? How can it fulfill itself? Surely it was not made to be dumb. Who will offer it a language? How pitifully little we do know of each other, and how we would really like to be known. I once had a strange friend in a little Iowa town. He was a veritable contradiction in character. He had a strong mind and a peculiar personality. He was reputed to be an infidel, though I never believed the repute. He died a suffering death from a carbuncle that fastened its painful teeth into his neck. I stepped up beside the cot on which he lay in great pain one day. Death was waiting at the door. He knew he had but a short time longer to be here on earth. He looked up at me with faded-out eyes, and said in a way I can never erase from my memory, "Rice, you don't know me." It went so deep into my soul that I stood quietly looking down into the face of my stranger friend with not one word to say, till some minutes had gone—then I said, "No, 'P. F.' I don't know you." Then it came back upon me, "Whom do I know?" Then I began trying to break into my own heart with the question, "Who knows me?" What a bundle of secrets is life. I stand here looking into your faces. What do I know? True, there are some things I know, that doubtless, if some of you knew I know, I would find out some more things very soon. But you are a great audience of secrets, sitting secure, and you know it. "The rich have troubles that to the poor would seem incredible." I think that is out of that searching book "The Pit." The poor are pinched by trouble which their poverty cannot explain. There are ailments which arise from defects of organism, slight deformities, unknown disabilities. I remember hearing Bishop Goodsell tell an incident about an organist who played in one of his churches with the rarest skill of a musician, but whose conduct was distracting because he was so lazy! The Bishop had lost patience with him and been very severe in his criticism, because he felt the young man was not honest with his endowment. The organist died quite suddenly. A post-mortem examination proved that what had been hastily interpreted as sheer laziness was a physical necessity because of a peculiar heart construction. Said the Bishop, "I then resolved that thereafter my criticisms would have to be less severe of my fellow men, or else my information would have to be more comprehensive." We can tell perhaps of many troubles, but the strange sense of bitterness in them all, we must possess alone. How strange this makes us feel at times! These hearts of ours are touches of an infinite, upon whose surface we skim some thoughts, but cannot guess at the depths, and the sounding wire breaks as we feel ever after it. We feel, and realize the strange sense of our own selves, but have no way to open it to others. In King Richard II, Shakespeare brings this vividly out. Bolingbroke speaks to the king. "I thought you had been willing to resign." The king answers, "My crown I am, but still my griefs are mine; you may my glories and my state depose, but not my griefs. Still I am king of those."

I need not force this argument further. Imperfectly put though it be, it is enough to touch your experience, and I am sure every one of you will have been busier thus far in this sermon with confirmations in your memory of the general con-

tention than in paying attention to the manner of
my putting it in these words. There is a bit of
indirect, yet to me unusually strong religious argument in all this. Along with the fact of loneness, crowds close to all of us the fact that we
hunger for true understanding. Our joys, eager
to find a sharing, have leaped to our lips in shouts
and laughter, and oft been quenched to find our
companions unable to understand us, and believing we were merely emotional. I was wandering
down the halls of a great art gallery once, and
stopped before a wonderful picture. It caught
my soul, and I was compelled to speak. I turned
to the nearest hearer and said what I felt the
best I could. He answered me with utterly stolid
face in a language I don't think I have ever heard
before or since. Our sorrows, yearning for com-
prehension, have been doubled almost by discovering that they simply could not make themselves
understood. This is as profound a paradox as
anything I know in human life. Someone has
said, "Man is only partially understood, or pitied,
or loved by man; but for the fullness of these
things he must go to some far off country." I
believe it has proven true in all our lives, that in
proportion as we have been made to feel we have
not been understood, we have reached out after
God. That is the contention in all this matter
to me. It says here in the Book, "If thou sayest,
Behold, we knew not this man; doth not he that

weighed the heart consider, and he that keepeth the soul, doth not he know?" And that poor lone man, lying on his suffering couch, torn by most pitiless pain, and touched even there by a keen emphasis of bitterness none could know, compelled to look up at me even as I sought to help him and say, "You don't know me"; that very experience of my old friend "P. F." has often proven the spur to drive men toward God. We want to be understood. We want to be known. If men can't know us, we turn our lonesome souls toward God. In one of his very strange books, Frank Norris, who died so unexpectedly before he had completed the plan he had but laid out in his literary purpose, had no finer stroke of real genius than when he made Laura Jadwin, a picture of despair because misunderstood, and in the desperation of that fact she drove to the very edge of the brink, in search of understanding.

The element we demand in the one who can look into our deepest souls, and weigh all our doings is holiness. We brook looking in on our evil ways by companions in evil, and still that confederacy we agree shall be on the ground, that we reveal as little and conceal as much as we care to. We would cease to share our feelings if we knew our real hearts were to be laid bare. He who is to search us through and through must be holy. This oft lonely human heart, longing for

sympathy and genuine companionship, starts out,
to discover the utter lack of such thing among
its fellows, and oft-times in sheer desperation the
discovery is made that this is just where the
friendship of God comes in. He alone can fully
understand. He alone can enter into all these
silent thoughts and unobserved emotions. I
would therefore turn this great human fact we
have been following now into a cry for God, and
declare my confidence that no human soul needs
to be misunderstood. What this world needs to
learn out of its yearnings and anxieties is, that
God is a "friend who sticketh closer than a
brother." The soul turns to find God, and dis-
covers that, strive as we may, we cannot quench
the hunger for God within us, unless we give it
God. When John Wesley was accomplishing his
last moments on earth, he flung back to those
who were yet to come on out of life here, just
as he stepped off the edge of mortality, "The
best of all is God is with us." And living or
dying that is our stay. God is with mankind.
You may sometimes be made to feel that you suffer the bitterest of experience because men who
judge you don't understand you. But forget not
thou, you have God. God comprehends us. It
is no longer necessary that any soul bear its bitterness alone. Though you cannot tell it, nor
explain it to your fellows, you can tell it to God,
and you need not explain it there. Listen, you

discouraged soul, whoever you are, and regard-
less of whatever reason discouragement may have
struck into you, no one need ever think he is un-
appreciated. What! you answer me, I have often
felt that little matters it what I may do, no one
will ever know or care. There are some, I know,
whose every wish and word seem caught as on a
thousand tongues and carried to a world of ad-
miring souls. But poor unknown me! There
might arise in my heart the finest feelings human
life ever knew, and no one would ever care. Here
I sit long, monotonous years through. The deeds
of my little hands may seem very small these days
when men are doing great things so constantly.
These days when the patterns of some men's conceptions seem woven on a whole world's loom, I
lack loom large enough to weave the design I
do conceive, and men judge me by the cloth I
turn from my tiny loom, and it is so small it
is tossed aside as useless ere it is straightened
from the weaving. See, the very world to-day is
spread across with great men's doings. I know
how this thought comes, and under it vast
hosts of noble souls are crushed. I arise as
a simple preacher of God to declare this
heartening fact, our God absolutely comprehends all that is in your heart. He knows the
will to righteousness. He knows the desire
to serve.

The commended message of God's Word to this

sometimes strange condition of life is perfect. Listen, you souls, conscious of separateness and loneness, you can have a perfect companionship. Hear it! O heart of man, busy at the rushing marts of a mart-made world! Even in your busiest moments, when the noise of grinding wheels or the crush of trying endeavors fill your ears with clamor, even then you can find the companionship of deeper life. Hear it! O heart of man, bounding with that strange wild, sweet music you call victory, when the shout of the people has filled your ears, and loud huzzahs echo in your soul! Hear it! you fierce tried soul, when the crash and wreck of bitterest sorrow has fallen upon you till you are speechless in suffering, and unconscious that any other could possibly divide your burden. Hear it! Hear it! O soul of man wherever you may be, whatever you may be enduring! God help me to say the word so it will fit snugly to every soul whose attention I can arouse! God Himself is interested in you. The recognized loneness of man must drive him to God. This I claim as God's own reservation made forever in man, and it cannot be trespassed on by any other. It cannot be occupied by all the follies and pleasures and sins men may devise. God stands guard over that reservation, and into it but one can come, and that one can come only on invitation. That is the vital evangelistic fact before every soul. I

address the loneness of life with the perfect
friendship of our great God and Father.

"The little sharp vexations,
    And the briars that catch and fret,
Why not take them all to the Helper,
    Who has never failed us yet.

"Tell Him about the heartache,
    And tell Him the longings too;
Tell Him the baffled purpose,
    When we scarce know what to do.

"Then leaving all our weakness
    With the One divinely strong,
Forget that we bore the burden,
    And carry away the song."

TOO BUSY

TOO BUSY

"As thy servant was busy here and there, he was gone."
—*1 Kings 20. 40.*

AHAB, King of Israel, and Benhadad, King of Syria, were at war. The battle of Aphek had been fought. It was a decisive battle, and Benhadad had been crushingly defeated and for fear of his life had hidden himself in an inner chamber in the demolished city, and had sent out messengers to inquire of Ahab what terms would be necessary to settle the war. Those were days when the terms of wars were settled on the field, and long negotiated peace terms were not known. Complications with other nations did not arise, and the whole issue was settled by soldiery and not statesmen. It was a custom among orientals then that the very first words which were uttered by the monarch whose terms were sought were made the basis of the negotiations. They believed superstitiously that the supreme powers took charge of the lips at such a moment, and often upon mere casual words was built an effective appeal for favorable terms. When the ambassadors came in before Ahab, they had robed themselves in sackcloth and sprinkled ashes upon their heads, and in studied manner they came crawling before him who absolutely held in his hands the fate of their king and their country. The very proud Israelite, much swelled with his victory, was not to be trusted just then to open a conversation in a manner that was proof against superstition and said, "Is he yet alive? He is my brother." That was enough. Those Syrian delegates snatched that sentence almost unfinished from the lips of the doubtless startled victor, and brushing the ashes of dejection from their brows ran with the word, and in an enthusiasm of interpretation that all the troubles of the war were ended so far as Ahab was concerned, and running gladly and almost if not quite singing it, I am sure they came eagerly before their hidden king, who awaited their report and said, "My brother Benhadad! My brother Benhadad!" When Benhadad heard the word he was bold at once to disconceal himself and came forth into the streets. And Ahab, seeing the swift interpretation put on his words, and imagining perhaps that he had made really a better speech than he knew he had, doubtless because he never finished it, decided to go even farther than they had made his words mean, and proceeded to show the defeated king the greatest honors possible. He took him up into his chariot, and allowed him even to make the terms himself. What did he care about terms anyhow? He had just won a great battle, and

that in itself is enough for any ordinary proud
king. Ahab was utterly drunk with his success.
He acts as though he were drunk with other
things also. And the long troublesome old king
of Syria was soon gone again back home, defeated
but not dejected, to gather again very soon his
purpose and a new army and start another war,
in which Ahab would lose his miserable life.
Ahab was driving home. He was swelled with triumph. Everyone knew he was the victor, and that
was big pay to a little man in a prominent place.
What matter the terms? It wasn't terms he was
fighting for. He wanted to whip the Syrians.
And as he came along, wrapped round in the
glowing comfort of his heralded victory, he saw
a miserable, dust-covered, wounded man by the
road side. The poor wretch from the dust hailed
the king in his glory. A king never likes to do
little things so well as when he can stoop from
a great height to do them. There is somewhat of
a genuine satisfaction in stooping to do a thing
that if we were asked to do on the same level
would offer no inducement. When a great man
merely puts his hand on a boy's head the whole
world hears of it, though it never notes the fact
that an ordinary and interested man had been
spending his very life in that same boy's care.
So when this wretched, wounded, dirty fellow
beside the road called out, Ahab pulled up the
prancing horses of his chariot, and the whole

parade came to a jamming stop behind him.
"Say on, sir," said the king. And the fellow
propped himself up on an elbow that seemed
badly hurt, and began feebly to speak, as the soldiers came near to hear: "Thy servant, O King!
went out to battle, and behold a man turned aside
and brought a man unto me and said, 'Keep this
man. If by any means he be missing, then shall
thy life be for his life, or else thou shalt pay a
talent of silver.' And as thy servant was busy
here and there, he was gone." Ahab was quick to
pronounce judgment. It was a self-condemning
act. The king's sense of military trust had been
touched by that wretch of the dust. He had no
more than uttered the word of condemnation
upon such faithlessness, and had not yet pulled
the reins over his horses' backs, when the crouch-
ing man in the dust leaped to his feet before him,
brushed the ashes quickly from his face, and
stood forth disconcealed. Prophet of the Lord
before the king who had failed his trust. It says
in the Book, the King of Israel went to his house
heavy and displeased. What a changed march
now! I can see the loose reins drooping across
those horses' backs. The proud form of a moment ago is leaning against the padded sides of
the rattling chariot. The thrill of victory seems
gone from the parade. Samaria made no stir
that day when Ahab came in. And a few pages
farther on in this account you will read of the

inglorious death Israel's king died when he was
again engaged in battle with this same man he
so unwisely set free that victorious day at Aphek.
By a sudden and unexpected stroke, the armor
he wore was pierced by an arrow. No one knew
from whence it came. It had been shot at a ven-
ture by an unknown archer far back in the Syrian
ranks. But they drove the king from the field
wounded to his death. And that is the completed
incident out of which I wish to tear this text.
If we could but see the events of life framed up
in the ultimate results they lead surely to, what
significance would attend them. So, knowing
now the results that hung upon faithlessness in
that day of Ahab, let us take the plea to pieces
and look steadily at its two statements.

First, "Thy servant was busy." Yes, busy!
How that word holds. That may be an old story
we have just read, but he was surely talking
modern talk, or we moderns are very much talking ancient talk. I am seeking now to get, in
an effectual manner, a religious word to you
busy folks who carry business as the sure shield
of defense from any neglect you may be accused
of. There never has been in all the story of the
world, a time when matters of really great moment were confidently avoided by men, and set
aside as though perfectly met and excused from,
with the reply, "I am busy," as at this very hour.
Busy! The world never really knew what that

word meant in the years of less strenuous life,
lived in days gone by. These are busy days.
What our fathers called busy would be a vaca-
tion to-day. Every invention of machine and
vehicle has been the means of increasing our ac-
tivities. We have flung our range of hearing
around the whole world. We have multiplied the
range of our errands with trains and ships. With
all these the range of the markets over which we
run our interested eyes has increased from the
single quotation our fathers had on the board in
front of the mill where the price of wheat was
chalked up, till now every man who keeps apace
with the world reads the fractional quotations
of grain in every part of the world, and notes the
price of the principal industrial stocks and the
price of money on every exchange. We are busy
all right. The old dirt-covered oriental who
framed these words would be dizzy did he but
imagine what his phrase meant when slipped
along down the centuries till now. We are slaves
to business. We post big presumptuous signs
on our doors that we are sure will defend us
from trifles, "Busy"! And behind that smug
sign we refuse to be bothered save with more
business. But business we want ever to increase.
There is no high level that is high enough. We
cannot conceive of such a thing as getting our
growth there. There must be a percentage of
increase that will prove the fair comparison of

other years. Business managers hold their positions in big concerns to-day by maintaining per
cent of increase.   The fact is, business holds
sway to-day. "Is the proprietor in?" "Yes, sir!
Whom shall I announce?" "The preacher." "He
says to tell you this is only Thursday!"

Don't understand me to say that religion in
any manner will counteract good business. The
Christian business man has no right to be second to any. I count him myself the greatest influence in the world. I almost envy a big business man, for the reason that his place looks like
such a high pulpit from which to preach. What
influence pours through every word the success-
ful man of business speaks! What emphasis
seems to attend every argument he makes! His
advice is prized. His counsel is sought. The
man who builds a pulpit of business success, and
then fails to stand straight up on it to utter
his clean message, is a terribly responsible man
before God and the age, of which he is so expressive a part. I am busy! I am busy! Yes, sir,
I realize that, but have you ever had any thought
about the real foundations upon which all you
have is standing? One of the outstanding business men of our city sent me recently that remarkable and influential bulletin of Mr. Babson's
on the "Churches and Business." The business
man had in his· incisive manner written across
the corner of it this word, "This fellow does get a

queer slant on things often." But Mr. Babson,
whose word upon business conditions and fundamental values is watched by a great many men
of business to-day, dared to strike fundamentally
into business for attention to the ultimate of
our securities. He dared to write his bulletin,
which is a subscribed for issue, and not a bit of
free gospel, but a deliverance for which he was
receiving pay from the men to whom it was sent,
as an authoritative advice, that the churches had
a fundamental value in business. He took up
the certificates of stock, and the instruments of
bonds and mortgages lying in safety boxes, as
counted as sure security, but were utterly contin-
gent upon the honesty of the men and women
who had framed them, who by an easily changed
phraseology, or even punctuation, could destroy
their value entirely. With such pieces of paper
we are in a weaker position even than was the
rich man Jesus told about, who in pulling down
his too small barns to build bigger ones, died
before he could get them built. He needed fear
only the angel of death. Our property could
become valueless before we were called. Our
securities are ultimately depending on the integrity of people. Mr. Babson dares to ask what all
this actually means, and then dares to answer
his own question by declaring that the value
of all our business and legal instruments depends not on the strength of our banks, but upon

the strength of our churches. The religion of the community is really the bulwark of its investments. Now, you busy man, hear this. Here is a word from one who spends all this time and thought studying the business situation and selling his advice to business men; Roger W. Babson concluded his investigation of value in the bulletin of which I speak with these great words: "For our own sakes; for our nation's sake; let us business men get behind the churches and their ministry. Never mind that they are not perfect. Never mind if their theology seems old. This only means that were they efficient they would do much more. The safety of all we have is due to the churches, even in their present inefficient state. By all that we hold dear, let us from this very day give more time, money and thought to the churches of our city, for upon these the value of all we own ultimately depends."

"As I was busy." O busy! Busy at what? Who was maintaining your values while you were so busy? What was it that made the dependable character of the men who lugged your gold and your bonds in bags along the street? What made the sincere character that guided the pen aright, that shaped the papers on which at this moment your fortune depends? The other day while the representatives of all Protestantism in America were assembled to plan for a great world

movement of the church, a cablegram came to
them from David Lloyd George, whose word we
have grown used to hearing with vital comment
in critical places of the world. It said this, "Even
the hope that lies before the world of a life of
peace, protected and developed by a League of
Nations, is itself dependent upon something
deeper and more fundamental still; the hope of
a brotherhood of humanity reposes on the deeper
spiritual fact of the fatherhood of God." Surely
we will not fail so great a crisis in the world
as this, with talk that will qualify itself around
our own little business.   Too busy!   Busy at
what?   It sounds like a good excuse until you actually measure it against the facts.   When all
the things of your business life are summed up,
you will find them stamped, "Temporal."   You
will have been spending your passion upon plas-
ter that crumbles before short time.   Whatever
you gain in this field you must leave behind.   All
the credit you have amassed will absolutely end
when your will is proved up.   You will have left
so many thousands of dollars in stocks and bonds.
Don't fail to get the right word in that sentence.
Thousands is not the word.   Millions is not the
word.   Dollars is not the word.   The real, big,
eternal word in the common question asked when
men die is the word "left."   He left it.   He left a
mansion beside the lake.   He left his great factory through whose busy doors thousands of men

go trudging to work every day. He left everything. And business, as we use the term in this
busy day, utterly runs out at the ebb we call
death, unless it be made the mighty opportunity
of eternal service. Here and there we meet folks
whose consciences have been stirred by the conviction attendant upon some shallow fascination that has been holding them, and they look
up troubled to ask, as they cling to some little
thing in which they have been spending many
idle days and nights in these busy days of ours,
"Is this little thing wrong? Is it wicked for me
to do this?" O the pity of such a question! For
when they have succeeded in getting an answer
which they think satisfies their own idea of right,
they turn again and give life up to the doing of
some silly piece of uselessness, again and again
and again, and think they are justified. I can
imagine poor, silly Nero, who sat fiddling while
great Rome burned. He dared to draw comparison. "Is it wrong to fiddle?" "No, of course
not!" "Then here I go fiddling away." And he
fiddled, fiddled, fiddled. But, my friends, the history of the world insists that that old fool of an
emperor shall be shown up in just such a shallow measure of himself. No one says it is wrong
to fiddle. But he who sits fiddling while Rome
burns must be measured comparatively. Let's
get proper perspective in our conduct, for we
must be measured before the life we could have

lived. The great searching question for you to
drive soul-deep into your conduct is, whether or
no in the things you are doing you are keeping
yourselves from doing other and better things;
whether or no behind its little bulk, the
vast privilege and dignity of duty is hid
from you. "As thy servant was busy," and you
argue that there was not a thing wrong in it
either. Playing, playing, playing. Afternoon
and night. Week in and week out. What of it
all anyhow? Grant your claim if you ask it.
What part, even then, is all this anyhow for a
man or a woman in a world as full of opportunity for genuine expression as this? Rome
may not be burning, but Poland and Austria
and Russia and Serbia and Armenia, and more,
are actually starving to death. Millions of little
children are going to sleep on starvation's very
edge every night now, and thousands of them will
not wake up on a very near to-morrow. If Nero
looks bad, he is not alone. These are not days
for folks to sit arguing small matters as to their
mere generic rightness. The text don't stab this
guilty man because the thing he was busy at was
a wicked thing. That wasn't it at all. He was
measuring trifling matters before real duty.
Busy, busy, busy. The word cannot be accepted
unless it qualify in importance, for it is some-
body, against whose interests you thus lightly
dare make your excuse. We are talking for God

now, and you cannot throw little talk at His claim on you.

For our second thought, and in conclusion, let us face what the result was to that busy man. "He was gone." The result of neglected duty. The resultant of false priority. The overwhelming consequence of misplaced attention. Busy on lesser things, he lost his prime responsibility. It is the calamitous result which came upon this man, occupied so thoroughly even with so good a thing as business. A man can be doing a thing that has not the least flavor upon it of anything out of place, and yet by that doing may allow his chief duty to suffer. I ask, "Is it wrong to play Jack Straws?" "No, of course not." "Then here I go. From this day forth I shall fish with my trembling little hook for the balancing little straws. Let come on all the mighty issues humanity can know. Let wars sweep the world to sorrow. Let starvation stalk the countries through. Let idleness close the shops. Let disease feast on friendship. Let pestilence waste the people. Let darkness and death come on. Let the Judgment come on. As long as I can see or hold out a hand at all I shall fish my life away after Jack Straws." Does that sound comparatively right? "As I was busy, he was gone." I have a right to ask you, What were you busy with? A young man testified in one of our meetings recently to this conclusive experi-

ence. He said he had been moved by a strange
constraint to speak to a friend of his with whom
he worked in a factory about religion. It was
Thursday, and he was busy with some little matters of detail that were pressing him, so he convinced himself that he could easily discharge the
obligation he felt by speaking to his friend the
following Monday. The young man could scarce
proceed with his testimony as he choked out these
words, "On Friday my friend was not at work,
and Monday he was dead." I am too busy! That
is a good excuse only, providing what you are
busy at is big enough business to set aside the
claim of the attention requested. The man in
our text was busy at matters that, had they been
measured against some other matters, might have
made out a case. But you can be so busy with
trifles as to miss the real ultimate issues of life.
The thing which happens in this story is, that
smaller matters of business that absorbed, are
dragged out in comparison to the supreme duty
of a soldier. He had failed in the supreme task
that was assigned him. Life must always be
measured so. When you come up to make out
your balance-sheet before the final test, you cannot bring out a lot of tiny trifles for credit, if
you have made utter wreck of the really great
purpose of life. What if you should come up
at last, having made complete havoc of your immortal purpose, and offer to God a few little

things you had been doing? With the wreck of
a soul before you, how pitiful you would appear.
I am too busy, Lord! I have a grocery shop! I
have a field to plow! I have an office to keep!
I am selling town lots! I am figuring on the
market! I am counting my money! I am too
busy, too busy! Well, my friend, your excuse
is perfectly good, providing the request you measure it before is in a comparative value. Let's
go fishing! I am too busy, I must plow my corn.
That is good. Let's go skating! I am too busy
keeping my office. That is perfectly correct. The
comparisons are fair. But the tragedy of our
day lies here, comparisons of value are forgotten.
Men are coming up to the eternal facts with mortal excuses. You cannot offer the excuse of being
busy at some little thing when eternal things
call you. Come now, let us die to-day! I'm too
busy, Lord! But all about us these late days the
busiest men we have had, have been excuseless
when the summons came, and they simply laid
down their big business and went away. "Too
busy!" You nail it on your office door and turn
to your desk as though you were secure. But
He who knew the relative values of things better
than all men beside said, "What, O what shall it
profit a man, if he gain the whole world and lose
his own soul?" With that question of our Christ
pounding at the inmost conviction of our souls,
we are amazed, all around us now, to see men

and women who seem content to lose their souls
because they are busy. They are careless with
God. We speak often and much of the sacred
trust of human life. We reckon some men's jobs
as trying, because they are entrusted with human life. We cannot close our eyes to sleep on
the great palatial trains, and forget the man
who bends from the cab up ahead, and keeps his
trained eyes on the glittering rails down which
we speed in the darkness. But we are every one
entrusted, and charged with an eternal soul. A
soul redeemed at an infinite cost and entrusted
to us to be consecrated to the service of God, and
at last to be set as a "gleaming jewel in the
coronal of His everlasting glory," or if neglected,
to find it overmastered by the tyranny of sin and
hurled forever from God, and as the ages wear
on to have trampled out utterly the long lin-
gering image of its Maker. That is the trust in
your hands, and it ill becomes any man or woman,
to face such a sacred matter and plead "busy"
as an excuse for its neglect. Nothing can be
too important to outbalance the matter of your
eternal life. Not long ago a great ship was
tossed and broken in a storm in the North Atlantic. Her engine room was flooded. Her
lights were all out. Her passengers and crew
were clinging to her great rolling hull, that was
the sport of waves and the target of the persistent
storms. There were no ships too busy to turn

aside from their important schedules and do all
they possibly could do to help that helpless ship.
Ships abandoned their destinations. They sent
out calls for other ships. They came from every
direction.   Ships!   Ships!   Ships!   Fishing
smacks off the Banks of New Foundland. War
vessels from far away coasts. Freight ships
from their patient routes. Great liners, racing
hundreds of miles from their lanes of travel.
They stood by in the storm. They sent messages
out to the anxious world. They got tow lines
aboard the floundering vessel only to see them
broken. They sent life boats out, only to see
them overturned. But there was never from one
of those ships the suggestion that they were too
busy to offer whatever they could for help. And
one proud day they brought all the passengers to
shore, and towed the old hull to port for repairs,
and a whole world, that had every morning and
every night been eagerly reading the last bul-
letins of those rescuing ships that stood by, to
help for more than a week, thanked God for the
rescue.   I am asking you men and women to
recognize the priority of religion. Stand square
up to your eternal obligations, and keep divine
perspective clear in all your conduct. You cannot be so busy as to find it a good excuse for
neglecting your Master's business.

THE RUN-OVER

THE RUN-OVER

"My cup runneth over."—*Psa. 23. 5.*

THERE is a sermon by Alexander McKenzie
that to me has long been the model sermon of all
the sermons I have ever read. I believe I am safe
in saying it has molded my thinking into more
lines of helpful meditation than any sermon I
know. If I were ever asked for what I think to
be the best sermon in print, I would name the
sermon "The Royal Bounty," preached from a
text taken from the Book of Kings. It doubtless
is due to the fact that one paragraph in illustration in that sermon deals with the text I here announce, that this sermon has come to form in my
mind, though it has been shaping itself through
a number of years. I have tried many times to
prepare a sermon from this familiar text, but
never but this one time have I tried to preach it.
I am sure I see here a truth that is vital to life,
if I can but find word and figure that will express it.

One day in the city of Chicago I was walking
through the great offices of one of the largest
industries in our country in company with the
treasurer of the concern, who was a friend of
mine in my college days. In passing along a cor-

ridor I noticed on the little desk of an errand-boy, who sat at his place awaiting his call, a motto that greatly impressed me. I stopped and carefully read it. The lad had printed it himself. It was done neatly on a stiff white card, and placed before him on the desk. "If you do only what you set out to do, you didn't set out to do enough." I said to my friend, "Who is that boy?" I was not surprised to hear him say, "He is one of the brightest, quickest, most promising young lads on our force, and the firm has its eye upon him." I have often wondered what has become of that boy. But his motto has been a constant help to me ever since. Where he got it I do not know. I have never seen it other-where. I have never heard it quoted by anyone. But I made it my ministerial motto that year, and it has dictated the temper of my annual mottoes very often since. I wrote it close up against this clause text from the familiar Psalm and felt its interpretation there. It is that run-over of life that interests me more than any other phase of life, for that after all is where influence begins. The part of life you consume yourself does not concern me very much. There is over in the earlier part of the Bible an account of the care God was bestowing on some of His people, when He was in divine patience endeavoring to get them where they could be entrusted to stand more alone. He was bringing them through the wilderness, and was with divine wisdom applying beneficence in a constructive way to them. Manna fell from the sky to feed them, and it was carefully prescribed that for each man there should be just an omer. Only as much as he could use. The enough of life. The omer never does anything for the rest of the world. It is entirely absorbed by the eater himself. It is a scientific ration. None of the great enthusiasms of life are drawn around "an omer for every man." That was a rigid prescription for the mere salvation of that company of people. Just enough. The strange thing to me is that just enough never seems like enough. I always like to see the table well cleared, but when I serve, if every dish is really emptied clean, I am a bit suspicious. It is after all the run-over that makes life rich and influential. I will be worth more to the world with a dripping cup than with the exact omer of personal necessity. If my poor little life never found a stream big enough to do more than simply fill it, what of it all anyhow? Just a cup full. An omer. Whenever you endeavor to make of that a life rule, what a selfish, absorbing, stingy measure it is anyhow. One of my very fondest affections for Christianity is that you cannot hold it all. The man who assumes the attitude of receiving, receiving, and thinks that is religion, has not measured the supply. Somewhere, in and about that idea, the real enrichment of human life is to be found, and it is the type God has chosen to express His relationship to human capacity.

This run-over of our lives is where we develop our actual value to the world. We sometimes call it generosity. I much prefer to call it the margin of life. It is that which lies beyond our own necessity. It makes up about all those finer expressions which go to grade our characters toward influence. That part of us which don't run over, our own personal consumption, the current expense budget of our lives, is the make up of about all our littleness and meanness. What I consume! What of it? "My cup runneth over!" Immediately some one else becomes interested in my life. Dr. McKenzie had a line in the sermon of which I just made note, which I have known so well in observation. He said, "It is the extraordinary beauty of a painting which enhances its worth. It marks the difference between genius and talent." I saw a fellow painting pictures in the show window of a store downtown one day. There was a continuous crowd of interested watchers on the street maintaining a never faltering expression of wonder at his work. He called himself "Wink," and threw paint in great brushes full at the canvas, and did it all very well. He painted pictures in ten minutes, and some of them he did not think necessary to spend so much time upon. Why be so particular anyhow, with a canvas only fifteen by twenty-five inches? Mountains, waterfalls, sky and sea! How he did hurl them against the receptive canvas! You could tell what almost everything he made was meant to be, and that is fair art in these days of cubists. His pictures were sold by the size of the canvas entirely. They figured it took about the same amount of paint to cover the same stretch of canvas, whether it be the green stretch of a meadow or the blue sweep of the sea. One foot by two and one half feet, so much; two feet by three feet, a bit more. No trouble there to compute the price of the pictures. Price marks were all printed and ready to be hung on them as fast as finished, and the marks were chosen by the foot-ruler. What the preacher was saying was that you cannot buy genius by the yard. You paint barns by the yard. You never quote art by the yard. I confess to considerable amazement when for the first time I saw that wonderful picture "The Angelus." I had seen so very many pictures of it, and had so long heard of the fabulous price it was held at, that I presume it had somewhat bulked in meaning to me around its money value, and maybe "Winks" tags on size of canvas had distorted my expectation. When I saw that great picture, I could have slipped it under my arm and walked off with it. It is not famous for size, unless smallness be a virtue in art. Millet's

"Dawn" is only eighteen by twenty-two inches, but it sold for eighty thousand dollars. "Winks" anything twenty-four by thirty-six inches sold for two and one half dollars. It is truly the extraordinary beauty and soul of a picture which gives it value. My contention is that for any man to be merely what he has to be, is, to say the least, little and poor and mean. There are men, and they try to pride themselves upon the fact too, as if it were distinguishment, there are men who would on no account ever agree that their measure should be in the slightest way too small to be capable of the description of honesty. They pay their debts. They have never stolen a dollar from any man. They are not wicked in positive conduct. They are merely stunted. They are solicitously careful not to be one drop too large. There is no run-over in life for them. They are the type of the man of whom Jesus told us, who worried because his barns were too small to hold all the grain of his field. He didn't worry because he needed more grain than his barns would then hold, but because some would get out of his reach. So he decided to build bigger barns. It was a purely selfish proposition. And God simply stopped that man because no matter how large he might build his bins with such a motive they would never hold enough. You who are day by day battling your hard way through all the multitude of conditions where motives get confused

and bother; you know that all the finer and real
rich things of life, such as love, and mercy, and
benevolence, and trust, and friendship, are things
you cannot put rigid measure about. These are
after all the real rich things of life. They tell
the best story of every one of us. They tell about
all the story that will remain. No man needs
dwell with pride over the fact that he pays his
taxes. You have to pay them, and because they
are compulsory you put in the basis of their as-
sessment, at the least possible figure. It is no virtue to pay taxes. Your benevolences are where
your character begins to find its expression. No
life ever gets any expression on self-consumption.

God has expressed Himself to us in this extravagance at every turn of His handiwork. "How
much more God," is a haunting little phrase of
Scripture which has been put close beside one of
the very finest expressions of human life, just to
let us know that at our best we are merely finding some feeble lisping of His ways. God's presence has everywhere blessed us with an overflow
of things beyond the cramped bounds of necessity. He never works as though He were doing
only what He had to do. How much it would
rob life of, if God took out of the world every
overflow of His Own ways. If He confined us to
a world made to the rigid lines of necessity. Just
full! Necessity has a stingy sound to me. I have
seen people try to pack Thanksgiving baskets by

that rule. I have seen these necessitous chari-
table workers. They send corn-meal and a square
chunk of fat pork and a sack of flour and a bag
of beans. That is substantial necessity. Folks
won't ever starve on that. It satisfies hunger,
and that is what we are out to satisfy. And all
this is good solid food. But, my friends, a great
amount of the real delight, and more than mere
starvation relief, of that basket, will not be accomplished, and I never enjoy the basket I send
myself, and I as the sender have some rights, unless I stick in a sweet-cracker, between the salt
pork and beans, for some boy or girl who may be
around where the basket is going. And if the
giver once gives way to the sweet-cracker, it is a
sure sign he has the right idea of baskets, and
will soon say, "O well, put in a few oranges, and
some nuts, and a box of candy. Well, I presume you had better put in a turkey too, since it
is myself doing this thing!" That's it! Seeing it
from my standpoint. That is the fatal omission
from so much intended charity. You look at it
as a matter only of the folks who are really hungry. The fact is that when genuine charity is
done right, the giver gets as much as the receiver.
God never made a world by the rigid rules of
necessity. I am so glad He did not have to take
up the task of creation on the cheapest contract
available. We could have a world in which we
could live, that would leave out much of the

characteristics we have come to enjoy, but which we do not require. This world is literally full of God's extras. I am so glad. I may not require them, but I surely do delight in them. They are the run-over of God. You cannot take up the hunt for God in any direction, where you will be able to avoid this same fact. He scatters with full hands. His whole story toward us is on the measure of the overflow. Therefore, when I try to find an expression for what He does for me when once He enters my life, I cannot do better than declare, "My cup runneth over."

Someone with the same dictatorial sense of economy which made the objection to the pouring of the costly ointment upon Jesus' feet, may dare to say that all this is an unnecessary measure, and must be classed as waste. A cupful would be enough, you say. You have not caught God's measure, even as Judas missed the fine devotion in that extravagance of love on the Master's feet. God is bound to give His people more than they can hold. About the only way He can gain an expression of Himself from man, is to so overwhelm him that the evidence stands clear, that no man in his own little heart can begin to hold God. Herein is the dynamic of Christian service, a fact too which the world knows and holds keenly against us. The Christian must not fail to give to the world the evidence of an overflowing life. We have made bold to claim a large truth. We have subscribed to the largest profession ever made by mortals. We cannot be skimpy souls. We cannot contain the measure. Our experience is at once doubted by those who hear us declare it, if we be caught going about stingily in our day carrying our little cups even brimful. We claim access to too great a source of supply for any such measure as brimful. There is no excuse for not overflowing. I took a stone jug to the grocery store. It was a half-gallon jug, and I wanted one half-gallon of sorghum. The grocer set my jug beneath a new sort of a faucet, and began to turn the crank and count, one, two, three, four. When he had counted off just a certain number of turns, and they were not many, he snapped down a little cut-off and stuck the cork in my jug, and held out his hand for my money. I said, "How do you know you have what I asked for in there? You can't see into a jug like that, and there is nothing in sight at the top of the thing." He answered me in mathematical assurance, "For every turn of that crank, a certain amount comes out. I have cranked you out exactly what you called for. Give me your money." And in these well-metered days of ours I have become so accustomed to meters measuring everything else, that even a molasses-meter didn't seem impossible. So I paid him the money and walked home with my clean jug. But I never liked that sorghum very well. Whenever I go and set a little bit of a half-gallon jug under a great big sorghum barrel, I confess, that as for me, I like to see at least a few drops of the molasses evidence around on the outside of the jug. It may be a sign that the grocer of to-day is a much more efficient grocer than the one I knew in my boyhood, but I am sure the sorghum of my boyhood days was much better than that we get to-day, and I should be a competent witness, for I used to lick the jug all the way home and know the flavor of the over-flow. This fact has run with its measure into life. We have developed a conduct which is in a mechanical way more exact than ever before. We know proprieties as never before. But the margin of your life is the measure of your use-fulness and service to this needy world. It is the run-over which makes you helpful. By what right do you dare not be helpful to others? What you may be able to consume yourself; what you may be able to carry in your own little cup, may be yours. But all the world has an interest in the accumulation of service that may find expression in the overflow of your life. You need it for yourself also. You have no right not to run over, with such privileges as are yours. Yet there are many to-day who seem concerned most diligently in keeping the balance of their cups so perfectly that they will accumulate that excess which sometimes is visible when that strange at-

traction molecular has rounded out and piled
up over the edge of our cups their heaping con-
tents. Shake the cup! What we need to learn,
in order to bring joy and enthusiasm into our
lives, is that really we were not meant to hold
all we could gather in life. Not that God ever
made any man's cup too small, but that He made
so much more to put into them than they can possibly hold, and that the finest thing any man, who
is blessed with a good plenty in this world can
do, is to go about with a running-over life. What
havoc we have made with God's measures by endeavoring to express them in our own tiny cups.
We have dipped and dipped and dipped, and
really acted as though we might reduce the supply to an expression of our own measures. Whenever the truth flooding this famous and familiar
text of ours now shall dominate our lives, and
we shall cease trying to find a measure for God
in ourselves, but rather shall allow Him to
gratify Himself in relation to us, we shall perhaps begin to catch at the significance of what
He was trying to tell us when He said, "How
much more will your Father which is in Heaven."

"My cup runneth over!" Of course it does.
Who ever expected me to carry about this world
any other sort of a measure of my God? God forgive me; perhaps thus far in life I have been
carrying about the world just a few sips in my
cup, and have been wondering why my life had

such scant influence. But, whenever I have
looked into a half-full cup, or even when I have
looked into a full cup, I have been abashed to see
it was a selfish measure and contained only myself, and the world don't care to see that in me.
Just as soon as I try to get God into the cup of
my life, my cup proves too little, and at once I
must carry an overflow. I went down under
Niagara Falls one day. Down under the huge
bluff of rock, and back behind the awful plunge
of that roaring flood. The earth trembled with
it. The overwhelming sense of the mass of great
waters that was running above me was impressive as I walked along through the dark tunnel.
When at last I came to a little opening where
I could step out beneath the great overhanging
cliff from which the waters were leaping in a
manner that has fully justified the claim of a
world-wonder, do you think I stuck out my little
pocket-cup to catch just a carefully dipped cupful, without splash or overflow. Rather I see
my tiny cup almost knocked from my gripping
hand as I, holding on to the rocks, barely touched
the barest brim of the sprayed-out edge of the
torrent, and as I pulled it back with dripping
arms I would have found that I had been unable
to hold but a few drops of what I had touched,
and the flood I had not gotten near to. O man!
man! what think you of God! Niagara and my
cup make poor little figure. You cannot expect

to go about this earth carrying just a cupful of God to show men. When once you set your little life before the flood of God, your cup runneth over, and folks discover God in you thus. If you will but consent now, you can be made abundant in your usefulness among men. God is before us not merely to meet our wants, "Not merely to gratify our great desires, but to make our desires great."

We have been on the trail of our real greatness with this very familiar little clause text. It is that consciousness we all feel, of an overpowering moral indebtedness. Not that we are trying to merely pay our obligations to our fellow-creatures. It is something rooted in the vaster relations of our being. It is the conviction that a contribution is asked now of us to the invisible interests of the universe. We are here, and we are expected to make a positive addition to the world's spiritual assets. We are in reach of God. Our cups must run over.

THE EXTRA BEATITUDE

THE EXTRA BEATITUDE

"Blessed are they who have not seen, and yet have believed."—*John 20. 29.*

AMONG the all too few things which were left us from the pen of an unusually interesting English preacher who was called to die while youth was yet making promise in him, was a small book of but few chapters, and titled "The Blessed Life." The preacher's name was Ainsworth, and his book, which I treasure greatly, is a study of the Beatitudes of our Lord, the remarkable opening paragraph of His great sermon. I count the little book the best interpretation of those beatitudes I know anything about. The contention in the series of studies is, that the very first note of Christ's preaching declares that the citizens of His Kingdom will possess real happiness. Let me quote just a sentence. "Christ could not possibly have begun with any other word (than happiness). He did not merely wish to gain the world's ear, He came to solve the world's problem; and that problem is always in its final analysis related to the question of happiness." That is a very vital fact for the preacher to realize. The world wants to be happy, and

245

the desire is perfectly proper, even though folks
do play the fool oftenest and most pitifully in
their mistaken pursuit of it. We all believe in
happiness. Jesus does not cross that fact. The
real need of the world is not that the quest for
happiness should be abandoned, but that it be
rightly and safely directed.

I am not divulging pastoral secrets to you
when I declare that the overwhelming percentage of all the troubles I have ever been asked for
some counsel in, have been those which arose
from an absolutely false leadership in the pursuit
of what had seemingly promised some happiness.
A young man, whose case made headline news
for all our papers several years ago, was finally
paroled from the penitentiary to my care. When
we sat down together to talk over life as it presented itself in temptation to a man, he told me
of the first steps that had led him away from
the life of simple, confident, Christian privilege
in which he had been raised, and it was of the
false fascination in pursuit of what he thought
was happiness. A young woman who took with
utter abandonment of appreciation, all the
beauty of a lovely Christian home, and tossed it
in wretched neglect until she was fiercely awakened by the gaunt fact that it was all gone, told
me when I asked her to let me know how such
a life could ever have found a place in her attention at all, that it began at the very same place as

the young man had said. They were on the wrong trail for happiness.

Doctor Ainsworth tells in his book of a most tragic picture he saw somewhere. It was of the last rough slope of a mountain leading to the close edge of a great precipice. At the foot of the precipice was a graveyard. The slope was packed with a dense crowd of men and women. Some were in evening dress and some in garb of toil. Some were in tatters and rags. One thing was common among them, they were all struggling to gain a foothold on the highest point. All were gazing upward with eager faces, where the filmy, beckoning, mocking figure of Pleasure floated just out of reach. The picture was called "The Pursuit of Happiness," and in that grim, ghastly, sunless canvas the artist had not painted one happy face. Not a smile, not a flicker of gladness; nothing but fear, and selfishness, and pain, and jealousy, and hatred, shone on the faces of those whose hearts were set in a false pursuit of happiness. I have just seen the picture myself in living figure. It is no new disclosure to any preacher. But I have just now been pushing a hard way through much wreck and ruin which false endeavor for happiness has wrought, and I have had to hear the searching pleas of those who have honestly begged for one more chance at life, having discovered that the common route to pleasure is a blind-alley leading nowhere; and I have determined now to try to say a word to folks of the eternal fundamentals of happiness which Jesus Christ has declared.

In looking about among these finely expressed beatitudes of my Lord's earliest teaching, great and good and comprehensive and far-reaching that they all are, I was made to think that He would certainly put somewhere, farther along in His teachings, an even yet more mature beatitude than any He would dare announce at the very opening of His ministry. And I was not disappointed in my expectation, for I found it right at the very end of His work, after His resurrection, just about the last thing He was to say to His disciples, after He had submitted Himself for an examination to the suspicious Thomas, and actually shown him the demanded credentials which He bore, His torn palms and spearrent side, and had seen Thomas convinced; then He said this great word, which carries the confident message of happiness still triumphant above all the world could bring, a word which I shall call the extra beatitude, "Thomas, because thou hast seen me, thou hast believed; blessed are they who have not seen and yet have believed."

That is a strong word in honor of an unsuspecting faith. It is a fundamental judgment. Every honest care, of course, is always ready to

show its credentials. But even ready to prove
ourselves, we have, and justly so, a bit better
feeling toward those who take our word, than
we do toward those who demand our proof. We
have made this into a standard national joke in
our country and fastened it upon one of our
States, and always receive the demand, "You
must show me," with a laugh that at least argues
it is not the great recommendation we have for
credence. We would not in any way be careless
of the obligation upon our faith to meet every
honest doubt, and the conduct of Christianity
toward doubt has always been tolerant. But
there is always a loss attending the demands for
proof.

I confess to just a bit of that feeling when I
get the incident of our text well in measure
against this demanding day of ours, a day so
often troubled, but a day of unusual self-confi-
dence. A day when so many folks go about the
world believing it to be a sign of intellectual
training and deep insight, to shatter the faiths
of the world, to trouble folks' confidence, to
worry people's trusts. In just such a day as this
I greatly enjoy to turn in here and sit amid this
calm conduct of Jesus as discouraging to disbelief. Jesus Christ shrinks no test. Thomas may
have disqualified himself for the very highest
relationship which could exist between his divine Lord and himself, by approaching him from

the suspicious angle, but he never bothered Jesus any.

Truth is always calm. It needs no defense. Error has forever been endeavoring to prove its own rights. Truth can afford to stand silent as did Christ before the great questioner asking Him "What is truth?" Error is clamorous. Truth is calm. This I prize greatly in Christianity. "Come and see," is its quiet, confident, open-doored invitation. There is no falter for credentials upon demand. But there is always a super-privilege for unquestioning faith. There is always an inner circle of experience for the faith which moves honestly and without the falter that waits on proof, upon the claims of our Master. "Reach hither thy finger, Thomas." Here are the nailprints. You shall not be disappointed even if you demand to put your hand into My torn side. I have not one single wound that is too precious to Me to be used to settle your troubled soul. But, Thomas, when you stand with your demanding fingers in the submitted scars, I will indeed be glad for you, and I shall count it high privilege even thus, under at least the colors of suspicion, to see you convinced! I want, however, to say to you thus won, and because you are won I can now speak over you a greater word than I could possibly say, had you not come along this limping way of a questioning approach, "Blessed are all those who have

not seen and yet have believed." Don't you see
how much more to Me it means for them to believe Me, than it does for you to prove Me?

There is a sublime dignity about a genuine
faith in God that scorns demanding proofs. "Except I see" is flavored with suspicion. It has
never been a great leader. It has attempted no
great campaigns. It has made no heroic sacrifices. It has been a mere recruit.

We have been of late months subjected much
to a morbid demand of a curious hope in immortality that has made bold to reduce the so-
called proofs of the "Kingdom Beyond" to terms
that disgust all the finer senses of faith. This
spiritualistic wave of interest, which has dared to
use the terrible shock of our great war as the opportune opening for a hearing unusual, has gone
about professing to show credentials of the life
beyond the grave. They have catered to that
anæmic belief in immortality which demands
some sort of a materialized proof for the immate-
rial state. They have not made the hope of immortality any more firmly grounded in the souls
of men. They have forever approached the great
secret of the life beyond the grave from the suspicious side that demanded to see and touch.
The immortal hope, that has been forever present in the hearts of men, has not dwelt there, nor
does it now dwell there, because of some mysterious thing our eyes have gazed upon, or of some

strange sound our ears have recorded. Jesus
said one day about some folks who were clamoring for proofs, "If they hear not Moses and the
prophets they would not be persuaded though
one arose from the dead." If you have not a
firmer foundation than the mere credentials offered by some supernatural manifestation, you
would not stand firm even with it. Genuine
faith is a quality of soul which stands on firmer
ground than sight. We don't see very well anyhow. Our eyes forever trouble us. I have a
hope for this troubled day of ours which is very
much superior to anything founded on what I
can see. We are drifting like a great rudder-
less vessel, without any course or pilot, and men
are turning with pathetic eagerness to Jesus
Christ as to the Pilot who is at home on this un-
charted and perilous sea in which we find ourselves, but behind whose horizons we know not
the way. You arise and ask to see the proofs. All
right! Reach hither your finger. But in that
very fact lies the sufficient reason, the status
of the spiritual life of this age is not as high
as it was in other days when men in leaping
faith were taking God at His word. The attitude of our day is that of suspicion. It will get
its results, but it will not produce an abounding
experience.

I happened, a few years ago, into the close of
a very remarkable incident which took place on

the railroad in Iowa between the cities of Columbus Junction and Washington. The train was
plunging through the dark toward Washington,
and many of the passengers in the coaches were
asleep, when a woman in great terror came running through the train screaming and throwing
her arms in wildest manner, seeming to say in
words scarce understood, that her boy had fallen
from the train. It was late at night, and before
the conductor could be found the fast-flying train
had gone many miles beyond the place of the accident, and certain of the lad's horrible death
on the heavy rock-ballasted track the conductor
told her it would be impossible for his train to
go back and find the lad, because no lights were
available on the back part of the train. There
was awaiting them in Washington, however, an
eastbound train with an electric headlight, and
the conductor promised that distracted mother
that they would place some men on the pilot
of the engine and by the powerful rays of the
searching headlight they would be able to find
the body of her boy. It was only a few minutes
until the train stopped at the station in Washington, and the mother stepped into the waiting-
room and was placed in charge of a doctor,
while two trained railroad men mounted the
pilot of the waiting train and took up their
watch for the little body that had been flung
from the open door of a vestibule as the train

took a sharp curve at a rapid speed. When the described place was approached the train was slowed down, and on either side of the track the vigil was made by those two watchers with care, and enforced by the trained eyes of the engineer and firemen peering from the cab windows. Sure enough they found him. The great train came to a dead stop as the engineer threw on the air full force, for all eyes seemed to see him at once. There he was, a lad, seven years of age, standing up in the middle of the track crying as lustily as any lad of that age ever could cry who appreciated fully the fact that he was hundreds of miles from home, and alone in the midst of the night, and his mother had vanished into the darkness and gone sixty miles an hour away. He was not hurt. Not a bone was broken. It was only a matter of a few minutes more till the gladdened train had speeded into Columbus Junction, and sent a message to the prostrate mother, declaring her boy to be alive and uninjured, and that he would soon be delivered to her in Washington, for a freight train was immediately ready to leave for there, and the boy was on board. The mother would not believe the message, and when they sought to quiet her by declaring that they believed the message, she said they knew no more about its truth than did she, and she cried out, "I will not believe my boy is alive until I can actually hold him in my arms again. I will not believe! I will not believe!" We do not wonder at her, nor do we blame her at all, but she only delayed her great joy about an hour.

"Thomas, because thou hast seen me, thou hast believed." The age of credulity is gone. We want proof now. And that is the summit of the spiritual life of our day. We get that much blessing, and we need not wonder that it is just a bit lean. It is not the greater blessing which would come by confidence.

I have spent so much of this sermon thus, because on the authority of this very last beatitude of Jesus I want now to say some things against the very best such a condition can do. Thomas does not for reward get the finest experience of faith. The man who demands his right to put his fingers in the wounds of integrity, reduces everything to so practical a stage that he loses the finer qualities of life. Let us turn from this lesser blessing of Thomas, to the larger blessing in store for those who having not seen have believed.

The great experience Jesus offers the world is not the mere satisfaction of standing with curious fingers in His wounds, but rather in that overwhelming experience which comes with His presence in our souls. Men in proud confidence of culture and learning have often dared to mark out the reasonable route of religion. If I can see Christ, just this particular way, then I will believe. It is Naaman come again. He has been an ever-recurring figure in religion. Men want to mark out God's ways. Poor old leper-struck Naaman, daring with the whitening evidence of his helplessness to presume to correct the suggestion for his cure. I always pity Thomas demanding God to do as he decides. By this method we throw away our faith. Eternity and immortality are not matters whose belief we can corner into a submission to our tests. "Except I see." Is it possible that such a brutal bold unbelief, which has no finer finger than its five senses, shall be made the measure of our experience? This is the spirit that has put a premium on unbelief, and sent morbid curiosity rampant through our most sacred scenes. I am not asking sympathy for folks who never think enough to have doubts. But the man who is really honest must adjourn some of his questions and not be impatient. "Be not faithless, but believing." Surely you and I, children of the dust, touched with a spark of eternal life, will not quarrel with the ways of a providence that is past our finding out.

"Blessed are those who have not seen, and yet have believed." All the other beatitudes were uttered at the very first of His ministry. This one could not have been uttered there. It would have been all out of place. Only after His wonderful life, and compelling death, and triumphant resurrection, was there a place for such a word as this. This is the beatitude of faith. I am not sure but that should have been the title of this sermon. The other beatitudes are concerned with principles of living. This is distinctly the beatitude of faith.

O Church of Christ, you are called to this high fact to-day. Doubt, and hatred, and blind enmity, and prejudice, and much more, stand thick about us now. This great truth spoken by our Lord must be made evident.

"Jesus, these eyes have never seen
    That radiant form of Thine;
The veil of sense hangs dark between
    Thy blessed face and mine.

"I see Thee not. I hear Thee not.
    Yet art Thou oft with me;
And earth hath ne'er so dear a spot
    As where I meet with Thee.

"Like some bright dream that comes unsought
    When slumbers o'er me roll,
Thine image ever fills my thought,
    And charms my ravished soul.

"Yes, though I have not seen, and still
    Must rest by faith alone,
I love Thee, dearest Lord, and will,
    Unseen, but not unknown."

So, while I walk by faith and not by sight to-day, that is not a continuous fact. One great, glad day I shall see Him as He is. When my much beloved father came up to die the other

day, he lifted his poor tired head from the pillow where the weakness of his faltered body had
kept it quiet for many a long tired day, and raising both his wasted hands he reached out into
the darkness into which none who stood near
could see at all, and his eyes that were going out
to this world seemed to kindle anew with the
glories of the next, and peering out there he said,
"The vision! The vision!" and dropped back on
his pillow, and no one knows what it was he
saw. We have heard it often. It is not unusual. I only specially treasure it, because it was
for him I loved. It has been Christian testimony
all down our story. Soon we too shall be able to
fling back our word, "I see! I see Him as He is."
Meanwhile here we are in the dark, and "Blessed
are all those who have not seen, and yet have
believed."

Date Due